Lessons are for Learning

Mike
Hughes

Published by Network Educational Press Ltd
PO Box 635
Stafford
ST16 1BF

First Published 1997
© Mike Hughes 1997

ISBN 1 85539 038 8

Mike Hughes asserts the moral right to be identified as the author of this work.

Series Editor - Professor Tim Brighouse
Edited by Sara Peach
Design & layout by
Neil Hawkins of Devine Design
Illustrations by Joe Rice

Printed in Great Britain by
Redwood Books, Trowbridge, Wilts.

Foreword

A teacher's task is much more ambitious than it used to be and demands a focus on the subtleties of teaching and learning and on the emerging knowledge of school improvement.

This is what this series is about.

Teaching can be a very lonely activity. The time honoured practice of a single teacher working alone in the classroom is still the norm; yet to operate alone is, in the end to become isolated and impoverished. This series addresses two issues - the need to focus on practical and useful ideas connected with teaching and learning and the wish thereby to provide some sort of an antidote to the loneliness of the long distance teacher who is daily berated by an anxious society.

Teachers flourish best when, in key stage teams or departments (or more rarely whole schools), their talk is predominantly about teaching and learning and where, unconnected with appraisal, they are privileged to observe each other teach; to plan and review their work together; and to practise the habit of learning from each other new teaching techniques. But how does this state of affairs arise? Is it to do with the way staffrooms are physically organised so that the walls bear testimony to interesting articles and in the corner there is a dedicated computer tuned to 'conferences' about SEN, school improvement, the teaching of English etc, and whether, in consequence, the teacher leaning over the shoulder of the enthusiastic IT colleagues sees the promise of interesting practice elsewhere? Has the primary school cracked it when it organises successive staff meetings in different classrooms and invites the 'host' teacher to start the meeting with a 15 minute exposition of their classroom organisation and management? Or is it the same staff sharing, on a rota basis, a slot on successive staff meeting agenda when each in turn reviews a new book they have used with their class? And what of the whole school which now uses 'active' and 'passive' concerts of carefully chosen music as part of their accelerated learning techniques?

It is of course well understood that excellent teachers feel threatened when first they are observed. Hence the epidemic of trauma associated with OFSTED. The constant observation of the teacher in training seems like that of the learner driver. Once you have passed your test and can drive unaccompanied, you do. You often make lots of mistakes and sometimes get into bad habits. Woe betide, however, the back seat driver who tells you so. In the same way the new teacher quickly loses the habit of observing others and being observed. So how do we get a confident, mutual observation debate going? One school I know found a simple and therefore brilliant solution. The Head of the History Department asked that a young colleague plan lessons for her - the Head of Department - to teach. This lesson she then taught and was observed by the young colleague. The subsequent discussion, in which the young teacher asked,

> *"Why did you divert the question and answer session I had planned?"*
and was answered by,
> *"Because I could see that I needed to arrest the attention of the group by the window with some hands on role play, etc."*

lasted an hour and led to a once-a-term repeat discussion which, in the end, was adopted by the whole school. The whole school subsequently changed the pattern of its meetings to consolidate extended debate about teaching and learning. The two teachers claimed that because one planned and the other taught both were implicated but neither alone was responsible or felt 'got at'.

So there are practices which are both practical and more likely to make teaching a rewarding and successful activity. They can, as it were, increase the likelihood of a teacher surprising the pupils into understanding or doing something they did not think they could do rather than simply entertaining them or worse still occupying them. There are ways of helping teachers judge the best method of getting pupil expectation just ahead of self-esteem.

This series focuses on straightforward interventions which individual schools and teachers use to make life more rewarding for themselves and those they teach. Teachers deserve nothing less for they are the architects of tomorrow's society and society's ambition for what they achieve increases as each year passes.

Professor Tim Brighouse.

Contents

INTRODUCTION

This book has two key aims:

Firstly, it encourages teachers to reflect upon their own practice and to think carefully about what they are doing in the classroom. It is something that we, as teachers, do not do very often. We do not have time to. Yet it is without doubt the single most important aspect of the job and somewhat ironic, therefore, that we spend so little time discussing and analysing classroom practice.

While this is not in the least surprising, given the ever increasing time demands of the job, it is undoubtedly a hindrance to our professional development as classroom practitioners and it does no harm whatsoever to re-evaluate occasionally our day-to-day performance and consider why we teach in the way we do.

Secondly, it offers practical suggestions for classroom activities that attempt to bridge the gap between the recent development in our understanding of how children learn, with the realities of coping with 8B on a wet Friday afternoon. Too often the gap between the theory of learning and the practicalities and constraints of the classroom proves to be insurmountable and is the reason why so many well-meaning books and inset experiences have relatively little impact on what goes on in the classroom.

This book is written from the perspective of a practising teacher - someone who encounters the realities of the classroom on a daily basis - but also someone who has enjoyed the privilege of combining a teaching career with working in an advisory capacity in the field of teaching and learning styles, as a PGCE co-ordinator and as an OFSTED inspector.

Consequently it draws upon a vast range of experiences and extensive lesson observations that cover the entire spectrum of secondary school subjects, enabling the suggestions for lesson activities to be firmly grounded in reality. Indeed all of the strategies outlined in this book are being successfully employed on a daily basis.

By the end of this book teachers will have:

- ☛ been encouraged to reflect upon their own classroom practice

- ☛ been challenged to think about why they teach in the way they do

- ☛ developed a clear picture of what constitutes effective classroom practice

- ☛ discovered a range of practical strategies to make their teaching more effective

The book aims to stimulate thought and generate discussion amongst teachers with the intention that the outcome will be to help them become more effective at their prime function: helping young people to learn.

Section One

A government-created dichotomy

In his 1995 annual report, HMCI, Chris Woodhead, argued that, *'Teaching methodology ought, nationally and in individual schools, to be high on the agenda for discussion.'* It is hard to disagree with this view. Teaching methodology is at the very heart of the education process and few would argue with OFSTED's assertion that, *'Teaching is the major factor contributing to pupil attainment.'*

There is currently much interest in the concepts of 'school effectiveness' and 'school improvement'. No issue is as important or central to the drive to raise educational standards as what goes on in classrooms, and it is no great surprise that recent research into school improvement reveals that an emphasis on teaching and learning is a characteristic feature of improving schools.

It is a message that we cannot afford to ignore if our desire to raise standards is genuine. The quality of teaching is identified by OFSTED as an area for action in 50% of reports, yet it is an issue of such significance that it demands the constant and urgent attention of all teachers and all schools. This is particularly true if we are to have a realistic chance of meeting the National Targets for Education and Training of 85% of young people achieving 5 A* - C grades at GCSE by the year 2000.

Given its undoubted significance it is somewhat ironic therefore that, *'The choice of teaching methods and organisational strategies is a matter for the school and the teacher's discretion,'* as, despite the abundance of legislation in the last decade, the 1988 Education Reform Act specifically precludes the Government from commenting formally on teaching style.

In short, teachers have been told **what** to teach but not **how** to teach it. While the vast majority of teachers welcome this professional freedom - indeed many, if not all, would balk at the prospect of being told how to teach - the lack of clear guidance as to what constitutes effective classroom practice is a weakness in the current education system. In order for anyone to improve and develop they have to be quite clear about what they are aiming for and, given the lack of national agreement over teaching methodology, this is by no means easy.

There is, of course, no single correct way to teach - almost everyone involved in the profession would agree that teachers need to employ a range of teaching strategies - or absolute definition of effective teaching. I do not seek one. Nor do I advocate teachers being told how to teach. However, without clear guidance about what is expected of them, it is difficult for teachers to improve and develop their practice.

As a teacher it is hard not to feel a touch of despair, certainly frustration, when HMCI calls for teaching methodology to be high on the agenda for discussion, as this is by no means a new message. The profession, and even people outside it, have been discussing teaching and learning styles for the best part of two decades. It was a debate initiated not by Chris Woodhead but by James Callaghan in his 1976 speech at Ruskin College when, as Labour Prime Minister, he launched 'The Great Debate' on educational standards.

The debate in question has been fierce, protracted and characterised by the entrenchment and polarisation of views. No teacher can escape a label: you are either a 'progressive trendy' or a 'traditionalist'. The debate allows no middle ground - it is black and white, with the labels 'progressive' and 'trendy' - whatever they mean - becoming more readily associated with the perceived negative aspects of the approaches. Traditional classrooms are caricatured by pupils sitting in rows and copying off the blackboard in silence, whereas with progressive teachers, pupils work when they feel like it.

Sadly, despite its importance it has largely been a futile debate, driven by opinions, with everyone - teachers, politicians and parents holding a view. Objectivity has been conspicuous by its absence and the dearth of systematic, academic research into effective classroom practice has been a serious omission in the drive to raise standards.

However, even extensive, long-term research programmes, although providing objective evidence on which to base opinions, would not themselves provide the profession with clear guidance regarding what constitutes effective classroom practice. On a micro level, teachers need to be clear about their specific objectives before they can select appropriate learning strategies. Successful lessons are those that achieve their objectives, yet at a macro level these objectives do not exist. Teachers do not know what they are being asked to do. Are we being asked to prepare flexible, receptive, independent learners, equipped for lifelong learning and ready to face the very different demands of the 21st century? Or, are we being asked to coach pupils to pass external examinations and in so doing, push our school a little higher up the league tables?

Until we know what we are being asked to do, it is simply not possible to determine what methodologies we should be adopting, let alone gauge if we are being successful. Not only, therefore, have teachers been left to decide **how** to teach, it appears as if they have been left alone to decide **what** they are trying to achieve. The only guidance has been the nature of the education reforms of recent years which teachers have been required to interpret and respond to. Far from making the situation any clearer, however, the contradictory nature of educational legislation and initiatives of the recent past could not fail to confuse teachers as to what is expected of them.

On the one hand we have seen TVEI with its active learning and student-centred approaches, GCSE with its significant coursework component and a style of examination that required greater ability to analyse and interpret information than memorisation and learning by rote, talk of lifelong learning and preparation for the very different demands of the 21st century, and the emergence of differentiation. Each seemed to suggest an approach to teaching that focused on the individual, gave increasing responsibility to the learner and encouraged young people to think for themselves.

This, however, was counter-balanced by the introduction of a statutory curriculum which many teachers still regard as being overcrowded; a need to cover the syllabus; an unparalleled emphasis on testing and assessment; published results and league tables; increased parental choice and a much heralded 'back to basics' campaign which encouraged teachers into whole class teaching, working through National Curriculum orders quickly and preparing pupils to pass tests rather than develop their understanding.

Teachers find themselves in a government-created dichotomy. It is little wonder that they are confused and it is this confusion that will continue to restrict their individual and collective improvement. Some twenty years after the Ruskin College speech, the debate rages on, and will continue to rage on, fuelled by opinion and given impetus by each new piece of legislation, until there is some clear, unambiguous guidance about what we want from our education system and, therefore, what teachers are trying to achieve. It's a bit like playing a game, not only without knowing the rules but with the goal-posts constantly shifting and with well-meaning amateurs cramming the touchline shouting conflicting advice.

For teachers this is both confusing and frustrating, increasingly so as they play the game over and over again with successive cohorts.

For the child it is more serious than that: this is a game that they play only once and one in which the consequences of defeat are enormous.

Section Two

Lessons are for learning

Let me nail my colours to the mast: lessons are for learning. They always have been and I hope they always will be. If I seem obsessed with learning, it is because I am and my concern is not with my obsession, but that amidst the hustle and bustle of the school day and the plethora of recent changes, the focus on the learning process can become less defined. Quite simply, there can be no more significant issue for teachers to consider as it lies at the very heart of effective classroom practice.

I do not seek a scientific definition of the word learning. I quite simply mean that children should leave a classroom at the end of a lesson knowing, understanding and being able to do more than when they came in. If we achieve that, we are doing our job. Consequently, as both a reminder and an instantaneous, if somewhat simplistic, self- evaluation, *'What have they learnt?'* is the question that should be on every teacher's lips at the end of every lesson.

It is a crude analysis, but if I am guilty of stating the obvious and oversimplifying the issue, I offer no apology as I can think of no more appropriate gauge for how effective a lesson has been, if only as a rule of thumb. It is also precisely the simple, unambiguous benchmark that is required as a salutary reminder that lessons should be all about learning in an era in which learning is not our sole concern.

We used to teach, now we cover Programmes of Study in order to deliver the National Curriculum. We either taught a good lesson or we didn't. Now we are graded on a scale of 1 to 7 in a range of categories that seem to omit only artistic impression and technical merit! It is little wonder that our attention has been diverted from the central purpose of teaching - learning.

If lessons are for learning, the following must be true:

- *Pupils should know more at the end of the lesson than they did at the beginning.*

- *'What have they learnt?'* is a key criteria for gauging how effective a lesson has been.*

- *'How will this activity help them learn?'* must be a key consideration for teachers when they are selecting teaching strategies.*

- *Teachers must be able to answer 'What have they learnt?'* closely followed by, *'How do you know?'* at the end of effective lessons.*

These are the questions that are uppermost in my mind whenever I teach or observe a lesson in whatever capacity and the more lessons I observe, the more concerned I become that there are a great many instances when children don't actually learn anything at all. Maybe I am guilty of exaggeration, maybe they just don't learn very much: either way it is a cause for concern. Of even greater concern is that on many occasions the teacher concerned genuinely believes that they have done a good job and the lesson would generally be considered by many involved in education, OFSTED included, to be a good lesson.

This claim is not surprisingly greeted, initially at least, with a healthy dose of scepticism but, before you react to it, put yourself in the role of classroom observer and visit some typical lessons with me. As you observe, apply the principles outlined above and bear in mind that the key issue is: *how is this activity helping children to learn?*

Lessons in which children answer questions

In these lessons the predominant activity is the teacher asking questions, usually to the whole group.

For example:

- *On what date was Archduke Franz Ferdinand assassinated?*
- *What is the capital of Peru?*
- *What is acceleration due to gravity?*

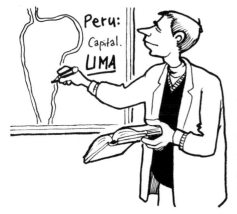

Ask the children - and often the teacher - what has been learnt during the lesson and they will invariably reply that: the Archduke was assassinated on June 28th, 1914; Lima is the capital of Peru and that acceleration due to gravity is 9.81 metres per second squared. In actual fact, the vast majority of pupils have learnt nothing at all, for in order to answer the questions correctly they must have already known the relevant information. The only person who does any significant learning during lessons of this type is, of course, the teacher who learns how much the group, or more correctly the children who actually answered a question, knew or didn't know about the particular subject.

In many instances, asking questions is an assessment technique and however effective it is in this guise, it should not be confused with activities that promote new learning. It can of course provide an effective start to a lesson by recapping and consolidating prior learning and provide the teacher with instant feedback about what has been remembered from the previous session. However, even when used for this purpose, we must be aware of the limitations of the strategy as only one pupil is able to answer each question - the danger being that his or her response is mistakenly assumed to be a representative answer.

Many teachers will undoubtedly point to the fact that skilfully designed questions of a more open-ended nature are more than just an assessment tool and, when executed well, can challenge thinking and contribute to learning in their own right. The contribution that effective questioning makes to the learning process is beyond dispute, my concern is aroused, however, when I see teachers asking questions that essentially assess what has been learnt in the belief that they are actually promoting learning. Often they are not and if learning is the objective we must be quite clear about how the questions we are asking are helping children learn. This issue is explored in greater depth in Section 5.

Lessons in which children spend the majority of the time writing notes

In these lessons pupils spend the majority of the time writing down notes, either from the board, a book or dictated by the teacher. Occasionally the note-taking may be punctuated by a brief explanation from the teacher or by a flurry of questions, but the fundamental purpose of the lesson is to transfer information.

The more lessons like this you observe, the more you may question how much the pupils are actually learning. They may well be writing down what they have already **learnt** - or if the entire class are writing the same notes, they may be writing down what the teacher thinks they have learnt - but they are not necessarily **learning** a great deal through the process of writing.

Alternatively they might be writing down information **to learn** at some future date. Often lessons of this kind are drawn to a conclusion by the teacher instructing the class to *'Learn this for homework.'* You may notice the irony of this situation. A professional educator is on hand to guide children through the complexities of the learning process, yet expects them to learn things alone, perhaps in unfavourable circumstances. This type of lesson is being taught all over the country on a daily basis.

Lessons in which children write down things they don't understand
Try this exercise yourself:

A mixed ability Year 9 class are studying the earthquake that devastated Mexico City in 1985 and have been asked to read a piece of text and answer a series of questions. The text reads:-

> *— the earthquake was caused by movement along the subduction zone. Here the Cocos oceanic plate meets the Pacific plate—*

One of the questions, arguably the **key** question, is;

> *What caused the earthquake in Mexico City?*

If you answered (as the entire class did):

> *The earthquake was caused by movement along the subduction zone.*

award yourself a tick. If you are wondering what on earth a subduction zone is, do not despair, for you are not alone - the entire class was wondering the same thing. At least, no one knew what a subduction zone is (I know because I asked them) but whether they were actually agonising over their lack of knowledge I am less sure. If anyone was bothered by their lack of understanding they didn't show it, consoled no doubt - as you should be - by their tick and the fact that they had managed to move an answer nearer to completing the exercise and an answer nearer to the inevitable *B+ good work* at the foot of the page.

This particular example may have been taken from a geography lesson but you do not have to look far to find similar examples in all subjects. It need not be during comprehension exercises that children can survive by writing down things they don't understand. It is equally common when children are writing down notes such as in the previous example. Occasionally, if you listen carefully enough you may just hear a teacher say to a child, or even a whole class: *'Don't worry if you don't understand it, just write it down so that you can revise from it later on.'* - Go on, listen carefully!

Lessons in which children practise something they have already learnt

The key purpose of these lessons is to consolidate learning, with children being given extensive opportunities to practise something they have already learnt.

It may be that after the teacher has explained to the class how to do long division, twenty calculations are set or, after looking at six figure grid references, the class are set ten locations to find.

There is a fine dividing line here between giving pupils the opportunity to consolidate what they have learnt through practice and application with simply repeating something they can obviously do. Consolidation is essential. So is applying knowledge and skills in different, unfamiliar situations. It deepens understanding and makes a significant contribution to the learning process. However there comes a point, and it will be different for individual children, where repetition is unnecessary and, at its worst, a strategy that simply occupies pupils as opposed to helping them learn.

Sadly, I observe a significant number of lessons where pupils are engaged in the same task, involving skills and knowledge they already possess, for large amounts of the time. The tasks do not increase in difficulty nor do they place the child in an unfamiliar context: they merely provide an opportunity for practice.

The fact that these strategies are employed by teachers is not, in itself, a cause for concern and there is little doubt that many of these activities play a crucial role in the overall education of any child. The concern arises when these techniques are employed for the wrong reasons and are confused with activities that promote learning.

Teachers have to be quite clear about the overriding purpose of each lesson or each part of a lesson and select the most suitable strategy to achieve their goal. Most certainly we need to ask pupils questions as part of the assessment process in order to discover what they know and understand and, more importantly, what they don't know and don't understand. Equally we need to provide children with opportunities to consolidate their learning and put newly acquired skills and knowledge into practice in a way that often brings further valuable assessment opportunities. Finally, part of the process of education does indeed require information to be transferred from teacher to pupil. However, a central argument of this book is that this can and should be done in a manner that consciously develops understanding, therefore leading to genuine learning rather than simply shifting information from text to exercise book.

Our prime function as teachers is to help the pupils in our care to learn. While it is clear that the amount children learn during lessons is influenced by a great many factors, learning is heavily dependent upon the nature of the activity they are engaged in. Consequently, we must ensure that the activities we employ in our classroom are those that will enable young people to learn effectively. I am suggesting that this is not always the case, and I am not alone. Based on many more observations than my own, OFSTED concludes that: *'Pupils may spend too much time on activities which contribute little to their knowledge, skills and understanding.'*

If you are still sceptical, reflect on the strategies that you frequently employ in your classroom and consider the extent to which they help young people learn. The procedure suggested on the following pages is equally effective when completed individually or by groups of teachers. The list is not exhaustive and teachers are encouraged to add to or amend it as appropriate. The key objective is to encourage people to reflect upon their own classroom practice and to generate debate over whether the teaching strategies that we regularly adopt contribute to learning as effectively as they might.

Step 1	Below is a list of commonly employed teaching strategies. Award each a mark out of ten depending on how frequently you use the particular strategy in your teaching. (10 = frequently. 1 = very rarely.) Try to use the full range of marks.	
Step 2	Give each strategy a second mark out of ten, depending on how effectively you think it contributes to learning. (10 = significant contribution to learning. 1 = minimal contribution to learning.)	
Step 3	Plot your results on the scattergraph overleaf.	
Step 4	Consider your completed scattergraph. Are the strategies that you consider the most effective in helping children learn the ones that you employ the most frequently ?	

Lesson activity	Frequency (1-10)	Learning (1-10)
Reading		
Answering questions from a book		
Individual help and guidance		
Copying off the board		
Observing demonstrations		
Dictation		
Practical work		
Answering questions from the board		
Writing notes		
Listening to the teacher		
Answering the teacher's questions		
Class discussion		
Watching videos		
Group work		
Individual projects / research		
Working in pairs		
Reporting to the rest of the group		
Talking to other pupils		
Educational visits		
Guest speakers		
Simulations / role play		

Lesson Activities : Relationship between frequency of use and perceived effectiveness in developing learning

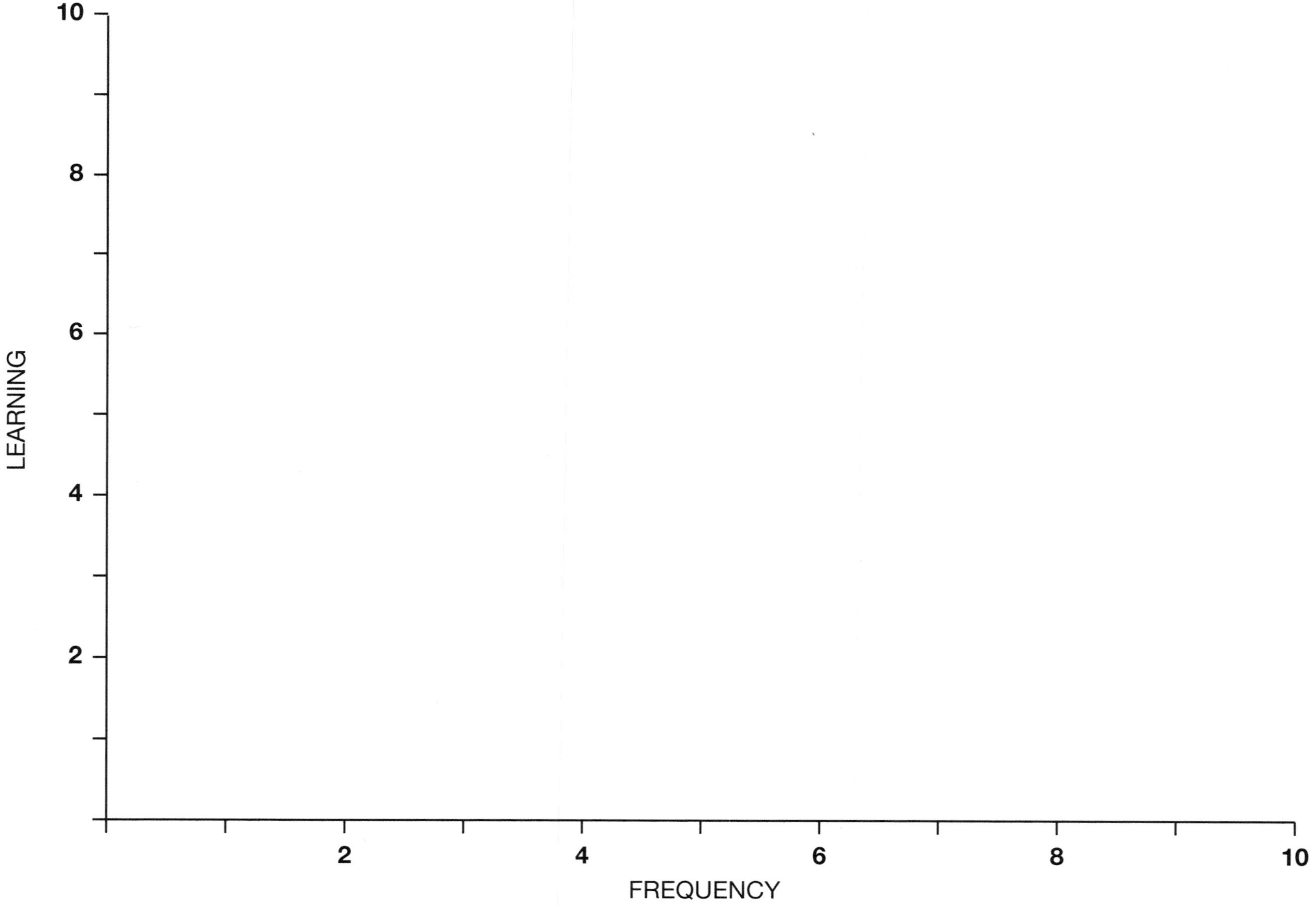

LEARNING

10

8

6

4

2

2   4   6   8   10

FREQUENCY

Any attempt to analyse the effectiveness of our teaching strategies would be incomplete without a look through the eyes of the pupils themselves. The scattergraph overleaf is an indication of how children feel about the activities that teachers ask them to do. The values are the average scores of a sample of over 500 children aged between 11 and 16 from 4 very different schools.

It is not intended as a piece of academic research but as a snapshot of opinion from the people who face the other way in classrooms. It is of interest, not only because it gives us an insight to how children feel about the various activities that we ask them to undertake, but because it often reveals a significant gap between the children's perception of what is going on in the classroom and our own.

According to the pupils themselves the following appears to be the case:

- ☞ The most frequent classroom activities are: listening to the teacher, answering questions from a text book and answering the teacher's questions.

- ☞ The activities that are employed least frequently are: simulations and role play, reporting to the rest of the group and individual help and guidance.

- ☞ The activities that the pupils claim help them least are: dictation, answering questions from the board and copying from the board.

- ☞ The activity that children claim is the greatest help to their learning is undisputedly individual help and guidance, yet there is a consensus that this is the most infrequent of all classroom activities. (see Section 7)

- ☞ Other activities that children awarded high marks for helping them learn were practical work and individual research and project work.

- ☞ There is more than a hint that strategies that are frequently employed by teachers make less of a contribution to learning - at least in the eyes of the pupils - than activities that they less reguarly adopt.

People inevitably react to this information in different ways, but regardless of the significance you attach to them, the views of children cannot be ignored. They are simply children's perceptions of classroom life, may not be entirely accurate and will almost certainly be different to a teacher's view, but they provide an interesting and necessary balance to our own inevitably coloured perspective.

How do children respond to the word *lessons?* In a word association exercise what do they say? Since 1989 I have conducted such an exercise with every group of children that I have worked with and now have the replies of well over 600 pupils aged 11 to 16. They are allowed to respond to the prompt *lessons* with up to 3 written words or phrases, the only constraint being that their response has to be instantaneous.

The responses, irrespective of age, gender or school are remarkably similar and, to me at least, of considerable interest. Incredibly, over 85% of the pupils who have participated in the exercise have responded with the word *boring,* with the words *listening* and *writing* appearing on over 75% of replies. Other common responses include *writing* and *answering questions,* with over 40% of children including the word *quiet* or *silence* in their reply.

Lesson Activities : Relationship between frequency of use and perceived effectiveness in developing learning

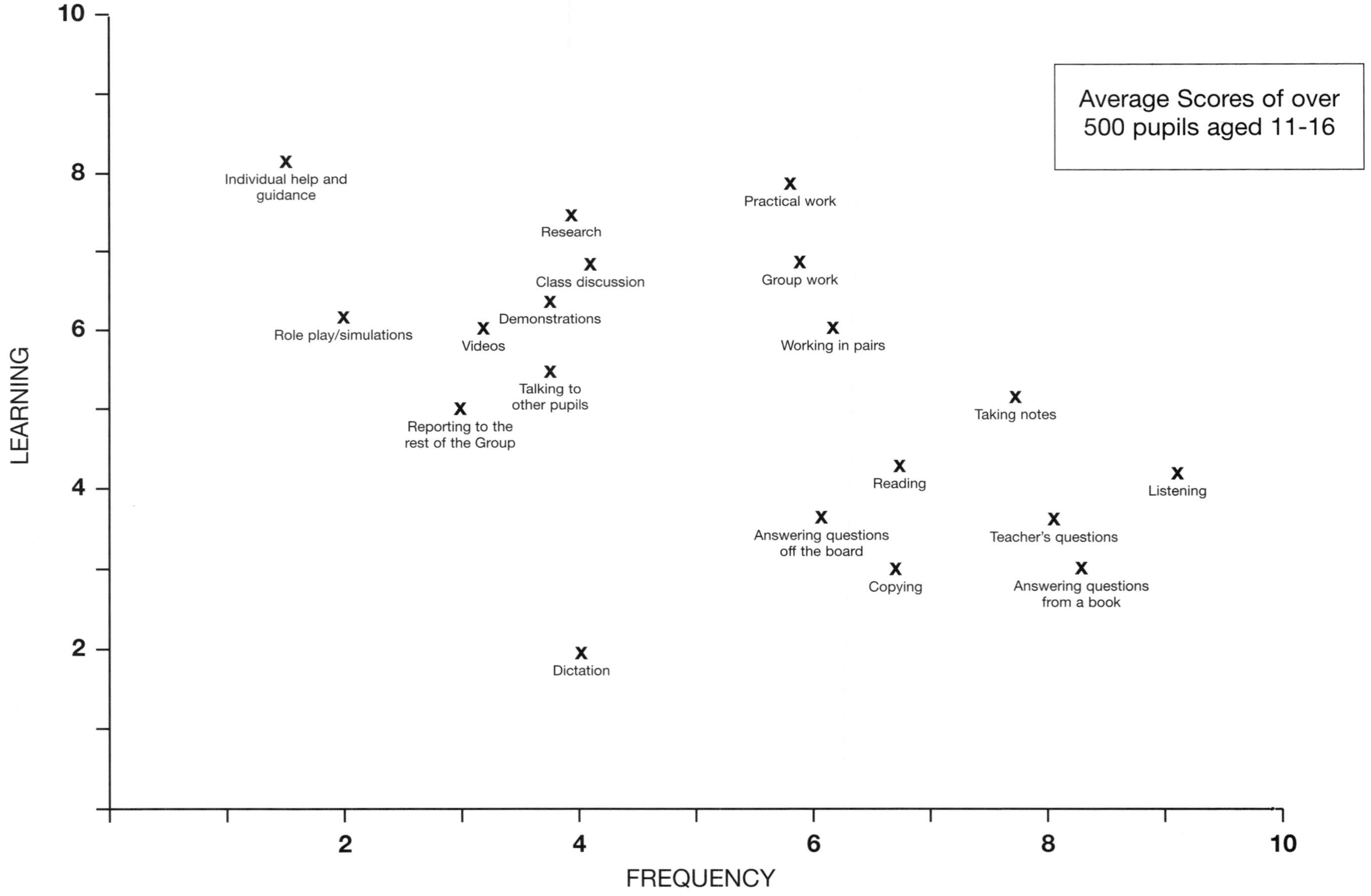

Average Scores of over
500 pupils aged 11-16
LEARNING
FREQUENCY
10
8
6
4
2
2
4
6
8
10
Individual help and guidance
Research
Class discussion
Demonstrations
Role play/simulations
Videos
Talking to other pupils
Reporting to the rest of the Group
Dictation
Practical work
Group work
Working in pairs
Taking notes
Reading
Listening
Answering questions off the board
Teacher's questions
Copying
Answering questions from a book

Many people may not be surprised by the responses: others will no doubt be tempted to dismiss them as insignificant. They are significant - their significance lies not in the rigour of the research methodology but in the size of the sample and the consistency of the replies - in that they begin at least to give us a clear picture of what is going on in classrooms up and down the country. There will always be exceptions but it would appear that children in general, contrary to popular media misconceptions, spend the majority of their time listening, writing and answering questions - and there is more than a hint of a suggestion that they are bored doing it!

The fact that children seem to spend a large amount of time listening, writing and answering questions is not in itself a cause for concern. The concern arises from the suspicion that, on occasions, these activities do not always contribute towards learning as effectively as they might. There is an opportunity cost involved - if they are listening, writing and answering questions, what are they not doing?

The clue lies in the words that are infrequently selected as a response to the word association prompt *lessons.* In total there have been less than 10 replies that have included the words *thinking* or *talking,* with only 4 children immediately associating asking questions with lessons. Of course this does not mean that children do not think or ask questions during lessons, but the fact that so few readily associate these activities with lessons helps us build up a picture of life in the classroom, as viewed through the eyes of a child.

The picture is complete if we consider that only two pupils responded to the prompt *lessons* with the word **learning** despite the fact that the whole purpose of lessons is to learn! Maybe we shouldn't read too much into this. Maybe it is precisely because lessons are for learning that we take it for granted, although personally I am not convinced. Learning is too important be left to chance, it has to be emphasised - pupils must be aware of what they are going to learn during a lesson and teachers need to ascertain precisely what has been learnt at the end of it.

This is not always easy. As teachers we know what should have been learnt - we know what we think has been learnt - but we rarely know what has actually been learnt, at least until we have had the chance to mark everyone's work. Even then we don't really know what has been learnt because we can never be quite sure what each child already knew before the lesson had started. The danger is of course that if we become too obsessed with finding out exactly how much has been learnt at the end of every lesson we run the risk of spending all our time assessing children and never teaching them anything.

There are a number of simple strategies that can be adopted that not only focus the attention of pupils and teacher alike on the need for lessons to be all about learning, but offer the teacher an instant if somewhat superficial indication of what is being, and has been, learnt during a lesson.

- Give each pupil a piece of paper at the start of a lesson (or series of lessons) and ask them to write down everything they know about the topic to be covered. Alternatively, ask them three short but key questions, while stressing that they are not expected to be able to get them all right. A quick scan of the answers as you wander around the classroom will give an indication of what the group already knows and, in exceptional circumstances, may cause you to modify your lesson plan. The whole exercise need take no longer than 5 minutes.

NB: A more thorough scrutiny of children's answers is possible if the exercise is conducted at the end of a lesson, in order to help the teacher with the planning of the next lesson.

- At the end of the lesson, or series of lessons, ask the same three questions again and ask the pupils to answer them on the reverse of the piece of paper. In crude terms, the difference between the two sides is a measure of how much they have learnt. As you peruse the answers make two piles: one pile of answers that are correct and the children have learnt what you hoped they would; and one pile of answers that are incorrect or reveal any misconceptions. These are the children that you need to see at the start of the following lesson - or even as they leave the room- to go over the work again.

- Ask the children to briefly raise a hand every time they learn something new. It is inappropriate to do every lesson, but on occasions can be quite illuminating. I first tried it with a mixed ability Year 8 class that I had been teaching for about 3 weeks. As the lesson progressed I became increasingly aware that one boy, James was alone in having not put his hand up once. I was aware that he was an able student but it was not until I talked to him after the lesson and discovered that he had indeed previously known all that we had covered and a good deal more besides that I discovered just how able he was. After this incident I observed him working in a number of subjects and was struck by how rarely he was challenged and how little new information he actually learnt.

Now set yourself two personal goals: firstly, to ensure that everybody raises their hand at least once and secondly, to see if you can manage to get a raised hand within 60 seconds of the start.

- The end of a lesson is often a time for hurriedly given homework and a mad scramble for the exit. Within seconds, attention has switched from French or Science to football, the lunch menu or choir practice and much of what has been covered in the lesson is instantaneously forgotten. Instead, spend the last couple of minutes reflecting on what has been learnt and make this the normal way for lessons to end until it becomes second nature. There are a number of ways of doing this:
  - Allow 2 minutes of silent reflection
  - Ask the children to spend 30 seconds telling a partner what they have just learnt
  - Write down 3 things they have learnt on a piece of paper
  - Sit by the door and ask each child in turn, or a random selection of children, what they have learnt during the lesson.

The same techniques can be used at the start of a lesson, as a way of reminding people and reinforcing what has been learnt during previous sessions.

If nothing else these strategies help focus the attention of both teacher and pupil upon the importance of learning. They need not be used every lesson, but on occasions they can provide an effective and salutary reminder that lessons are indeed for learning!

Children learn effectively when ...

OFSTED recommends that schools should enquire whether all teachers have adequate understanding of how children learn. It is good advice, for understanding how children learn is the key to effective classroom practice and as such should provide the focus for our attention and research.

Instead we debate, in a strangely circular motion, the relative merits of mixed ability teaching, of grouping pupils by ability or by gender, of organising classes to work in small groups compared to teaching the class as a whole. As a profession we have allowed the teaching and learning debate to be hijacked, condemning it to a low level bar room argument that consistently misses the point. While there may be other issues that merit consideration, they are but side-shows to the key issue of how children learn. However they are grouped, and whichever way the class is organised, it is the activities that children are engaged in that will determine how much they will learn and therefore how effective a lesson is.

This should be firmly in our mind when we are planning our lessons and selecting our strategies. If we ask ourselves, *'What have they learnt?'* at the end of a lesson, we must surely be asking, *'How is this activity going to help them learn?'* at the beginning. We are not searching for a single answer. Whether pupils are working in small groups, writing in silence or listening to the teacher does not matter - different strategies are appropriate for different objectives and all teachers will have their personal preferences - providing the question, *'How is this helping them learn?'* can be answered satisfactorily. We are searching for principles, not teaching styles, and must not let deep-seated prejudices colour our judgement.

There are no easy answers. Learning is undoubtedly a complex business and dependent upon a multitude of inter-related factors. Our understanding of how the human brain works is increasing all the time and the messages of recent developments in brain science are beginning to filter through the education world. Too often, however, the gap between the theory of learning and the practicalities and constraints of the classroom proves to be insurmountable and is the reason why so many invaluable discoveries into the working of the brain are so rarely applied in the classroom.

There is an understandable inclination to be wary of what some teachers regard as overcomplicating the business of teaching. Yet this need not be so. Advances in brain science do not pose us with new problems but can help to make our teaching even more effective. Consider the way in which you learn effectively and apply those principles to your teaching. Better still, consider the conditions that are least conducive to learning - often this is easier - and try to avoid them. (This is one of the INSET activities outlined in Section 8.) Simply thinking about and debating how children learn is likely to bring benefits for, if nothing else, it focuses our attention on what is undoubtedly the key issue.

How would you complete the sentence: *'Children learn effectively when —-?'* Complete it, stick a copy to your desk and ensure that you have created the conditions that children need to learn effectively during every lesson you teach. There is no solitary solution. Effective learning is undoubtedly the result of, and dependent upon, many factors. In some respects it is like a recipe and teachers, like any chef, need to know not only the ingredients but when, and in what quantities, to use them.

The recipe that is stuck to my desk and which is my contribution to the teaching and learning debate reads as follow:

Children learn effectively when —-

- ☛ *they are interested in and enjoy what they are doing - lessons are memorable*

- ☛ *they ask, as opposed to answer, questions*

- ☛ *they are challenged to think about the work they are doing*

- ☛ *they understand what they are learning*

- ☛ *they receive individual help and attention*

There are, of course, a handful of especially talented chefs who have the indefinable ability to take the same basic ingredients as their colleagues, but use and turn them into something special. Their secret lies both in the blend and the additional herbs and spices

they throw in the pot to give the finished product their own distinct and special flavour. Theirs is a natural talent, honed with experience, for others to admire and to try in vain to emulate.

Similarily with some teachers, it is apparent that, as the flavour of the dish depends in no small measure on the skill of the person who cooked it, we cannot divorce the personal qualities of the teacher with the quality of the teaching. Some teachers are competent, others are inspirational. A few are blessed with a natural and indefinable ability to simplify the most difficult concept and to make even the most mundane seem fascinating. No book or course can create them; I do not try to. I am simply trying to identify the basic ingredients - ingredients that they garnish with patience, humour and sheer personality -that they use.

Subsequent sections explore each of the components of effective learning in greater depth and outline a range of practical classroom strategies that are specifically designed to enhance the **learning** experience of all children.

'What is education if not enjoyment?'   Bruner

There is near universal agreement that lessons should ideally be interesting, enjoyable and memorable, with all teachers well aware of the correlation between achievement and motivation. Many of us find ourselves teaching as a direct result of being taught by an inspirational and enthusiastic teacher when we were at school who not only ignited our interest in our subject and sparked our desire to join the profession, but significantly influences the way in which we perform in the classroom.

Enjoyment is a factor of effective classroom practice that cannot, of course, be quantified - partly because it is impossible to isolate the impact of enjoyment on attainment - and it is not always clear if children enjoy a subject because they are good at it or if they become good at it because they enjoy it. This matters not. What is significant is that the link between motivation and achievement is as indisputable as it is difficult to define and measure.

These sentiments are neither surprising nor contentious. There are few adults, never mind children, who would not readily admit to working harder at things they enjoy and are interested in compared to things they find tedious. All teachers know that if they can get a class or an individual interested in the work they are doing then half the battle has been won. Children who are interested in what they are doing work harder and are therefore more likely to achieve and do well. The praise they receive for their success acts as further motivation and a self-perpetuating upward spiral of effort, success and praise is put into effect. It is a spiral that brings undoubted gains, not only in terms of academic attainment, but also the spin-off benefit of improved behaviour and the likelihood of serious discipline problems being vastly reduced.

The vigour with which we must strive to create this situation should only be matched by our efforts to prevent the downward spiral coming into effect. When bored children stop trying, low attainment, de-motivation and potential discipline problems are the inevitable consequences. Experience tells us it is a downward spiral that is hard to break. I often refer to it as the 'O' factor, as it is the difference between children coming to a lesson thinking, *'Oh God, it's geography!'* as opposed to *'Oh good, it's geography!'*

It appears that this is an issue that, for once, teachers and OFSTED can agree upon, with both versions of the framework recognising the significance of interesting pupils in their work. One of the evaluation criteria that indicated the quality of learning in the original framework was, *'Attitudes to learning - including motivation and interest,'* while the revised handbook requires inspectors to look for evidence of, *'Pupils' involvement in and enjoyment of learning.'* HMCI, Chris Woodhead, endorsed this point in his 1995 annual report by asserting that lessons that were judged to be 'unsatisfactory' or 'poor' - and approaching 20% of lessons observed in Key Stages 3 and 4 fell into this category - and were, among other things, *'boring'.*

His view that boring lessons are unsatisfactory would be unlikely to meet with disagreement from children of any age. Ask any group of pupils to write down what makes a good lesson and *'interesting'* will appear top, or near the top, of everyone's list. Some may prefer written work to discussion, some like working in groups while others favour working alone, but there is one thing they all agree on irrespective of age, ability or where they live - lessons should be interesting!

All students training to be teachers should have the opportunity, under controlled conditions, to talk with a group of children about what makes a good teacher and the type of lessons that they enjoy. I say student teachers because asking pupils about their opinions is something that teachers tend to shy away from after they have qualified, but it is an exercise that be equally beneficial for the most experienced practitioner. It needs to be handled sensitively and professionally, possibly involving a third party or questionnaire, and should not be personalised in any way, but when done well it can make an important contribution to developing an individual's classroom practice.

Teachers and students who have gone through this process are left in absolutely no doubt that children want lessons that are interesting and strive to create this interest with renewed determination. For more experienced teachers it can prove to be a salutary reminder of the enthusiasm and ideals with which they embarked on their careers before the frustration and fatigue of their daily routine, excessive workload and lack of resources took their toll on even the best of intentions.

While this is clearly an issue that requires individual reflection, there is a suspicion that at a macro level there are too many lessons that ironically fall some way short of the interesting, enjoyable occasions that we all agree they should be. It is this suspicion that is my motive for highlighting an issue that many may consider little more than stating the obvious.

That is certainly the conclusion that one would be tempted to draw from the overwhelming number of pupils who respond to the word association prompt with 'boring'. It is a crude analysis and as a research method may lack something in rigour and reliability, but it is both the vast numbers of pupils who claim to find their lessons boring and the consistency of this view, irrespective of age, that is significant and, if an accurate reflection, a cause for considerable concern. If nothing else it provides us with a snapshot of opinion from the people on the receiving end of our lessons and, if our desire to make our classroom practice more effective is genuine, it would be foolish and complacent to discount it.

Not suprisingly, the fact that children are often bored in lessons becomes more apparent as they get older as boredom increasingly leads to disruptive behaviour. I cannot have been the first young teacher to have been told by more experienced colleagues that Year 9 pupils, or the 3rd Years as they were then, are the most difficult to teach as they have 'switched off' but cannot yet be coerced into working by the prospect of looming examinations. Nor can I have been the only one to have wondered why successive generations of children 'switch off' in their early teens and the extent to which this gradual reduction in interest is, as puberty, an inevitable part of growing up, or whether it has rather more to do with the experiences they receive during the early years of secondary education.

Inevitably these observations are confined to generalisations and with any generalisation there will be *notable* exceptions. All teachers will have their own tale to tell and their personal experiences will inevitably determine their response to the suggestion that many children are bored in school. Many, I suspect, will identify at least an element of truth in the suggestion that a significant number of children take less and less interest in lessons, as they get older.

I do not seek to provoke individual indignation, simply promote collective reflection on an issue that is surely worthy. Sadly, worthy or not, this is not an issue that features regularly on departmental agendas or on INSET programmes and few will have considered it in any depth other than informally. It would appear that whether or not children enjoy lessons and find them interesting - a factor that so many consider significant if classroom practice is to be effective - is something that we leave almost entirely to chance!

It is almost as if we assume that all teachers have an inherent ability to be interesting. Some undoubtedly have, others - cast your mind back to your own education - clearly have not. Many desperately want to be but are unsure how. Whichever category you find yourself in, investing time in considering how the gap between the stimulating occasions that we want lessons to be and the lacklustre events children seem to find them, can at worst do no harm, while at best can propel your classes on an upward spiral of increased motivation and effort. It an investment well worth making.

On a personal level, this apparent gap between what we all agree lessons should be like and what happens in reality does not surprise me. I was bored as a pupil, and although there were one or two notable exceptions, generally found the techniques employed by many teachers to be tedious and lacking in challenge. Although my school days are long over, the memories of endless comprehensions, copying notes off the board, worksheet after worksheet, and listening, or at least pretending to listen, to the teacher have not faded.

Then, as now, I found no reason to disagree with the HMI view that,

More than anything else teaching methods affect the response of the pupils and determine whether they are interested, motivated and involved in the lesson in such a way as to be engaged in good learning

and the fact that this was written in 1979 in no way invalidates it.

Certainly some individuals have been blessed with the lively, outgoing personality that people find naturally engaging, but while that will go a long way to helping children enjoy their lessons, it will not ensure it. Similarly, those of us who cannot juggle or manage to maintain a barrage of jokes are not precluded from teaching lessons that motivate and interest. Children are not bored simply because the teacher lacks charisma, but because of the nature of the activities they are asked to undertake.

Children, like adults, will quickly become bored if they are not fully engaged in the learning activity. They need to be challenged and stimulated by the tasks, irrespective of the subject or topic they are studying. Inevitably even the most conscientious student will become bored if they spend too much time listening to the teacher, answering questions from books or writing page after page of notes. Yet, judging by the scattergraph in Section 2, these are exactly the kind of activities that children are engaged in on a regular basis and, if this research bears any resemblance at all to what is going on in classrooms up and down the country, no one should be in the least surprised that children are bored.

In many respects it would appear that classrooms have changed rather less than many on the outside of education would have us believe since I sat and passively received information all those years ago. Superficially they may have changed - children may now sit in groups where previously they sat in rows; video recorders have replaced slide projectors; and many blackboards have turned white, but whether the learning activities that children are engaged in have fundamentally altered, I am less sure.

The children who took part in this research claim that they still spend a large amount of time, as I did, answering questions from books, writing down information and listening to the teacher. Indeed, they would appear to spend more time listening than any other activity, and listening is an activity that young people can only do for so long, however inspirational and entertaining the teacher.

If I was generally bored as a pupil then the feeling was particularly acute in maths, physics and, to a lesser extent, geography. It was not that my maths and physics teachers were exceptionally uninspiring or that the tasks we were required to complete especially tedious. I quite simply did not understand the work.

Seemingly nothing in these subjects came easily to me and, although I often managed to grasp the point after covering it 3 or 4 times, I was rarely afforded the luxury of the multiple explanations that I required, largely because the rest of the group was ready to move on to new material long before I was ready. Not only was the pace of the learning too fast for me, the lessons were conducted in a language whose depth and complexity, while entirely appropriate for the majority of the group, was far beyond my comprehension. Indeed it is doubtful if the subjects would have been any more of a mystery to me if the lessons had been conducted in Chinese!

It is little wonder that the enthusiasm that I brought in abundance from primary school, which reached a crescendo as I first entered the exhilarating world of a science laboratory should have been replaced by a combination of frustration and boredom bordering on resentment when I quickly realised that maths and science lessons were not for learning but for surviving in the vain hope that my inadequacies would not be cruelly exposed to my contemporaries. If I managed that, which I very much doubt, it had far more to do with help from sympathetic friends and the animal-like survival instincts that all pupils possess in abundance, than as a result of any conscious strategy of my teachers, all of whom appeared oblivious to my plight.

Conversely, my problem in geography was not that I didn't understand but that I understood new material rather quicker than the rest of my class. Geography came naturally to me and, in the early years of secondary education at least, posed no great problems. Indeed my insatiable appetite for information about anything remotely geographical meant that I had often already discovered much of the material that we were being taught prior to the lesson. Consequently I began to find the work less of a challenge -dare I say easy - as I got older and, to my amazement, I began to find geography lessons, if not boring in the same way that I found maths and physics, less stimulating than when I was young.

This frustration was compounded by the fact that I always seemed to finish an exercise well in advance of anybody else and although I was desperate to move on to more demanding tasks, I was frequently forced to wait for others to catch up. There was always a good reason, at least according to the teacher, for me not to move on alone - it always seemed that the end of the lesson was only a few minutes away or we were about to embark on an exciting new topic next lesson - and so I spent a significant proportion of each geography lesson being encouraged to check my work for mistakes. Not surprisingly, gazing out of the window seemed a more attractive option!

Occasionally my geography teacher was moved to give me some additional work, exercises that are often referred to as 'extension material'. It a misleading phrase, however, as only rarely was I extended in the sense that my knowledge and understanding were deepened or even broadened. All too often I was rewarded for successfully completing my work with tasks that were trivial in the extreme and exactly the opposite of the type of challenge that I had clearly demonstrated I was ready for. It may have been more productive than looking out of the window - but only just!

It was not just that I was bored, I wasn't learning very much either. If the odd 5 minutes can be justified in isolation, what must have amounted to well over 30 lessons during my formal education clearly cannot. To those who are smiling quietly to themselves and feel that I would have been better served if I had been taught in an group setted by ability - I was!

There is a natural temptation, particularly I suspect among teachers who privately accept that their lessons are less than stimulating, to attempt to justify their rather colourless approach and, almost inevitably, their justifications invariably begin with the phrase, 'Ah, but'. The common 'Ah, buts' are described in Section 9, the gist of the argument being that interesting lessons are all very well but there really isn't time to stimulate children and cover an excessively overcrowded National Curriculum and, in any case, the more interesting you try and make a lesson the more you run the risk of behavioural problems.

It is a flimsy defence however and one that is all too easy to hide behind. Lessons that both capture and sustain the interest of children need not be any more time demanding than more mundane alternatives, although if this was the price for children being motivated, working harder and learning more, then I for one would consider it well worth paying. Nor do activities that fully engage pupils in their learning necessarily lead to a breakdown in control. These are the misconceptions that arise from the polemic view that the only alternative to children sitting listening or writing are small groups of pupils huddled together chatting about anything other than the task in hand.

There is, of course, not one correct way to make lessons interesting and generations of teachers have approached and accomplished the challenge in a variety of ways. It is undeniably and inextricably linked to individual personality and manner, but by no means dependent upon it. It is not simply the teacher that pupils must find interesting for learning to be effective, although that is clearly a bonus, but the lesson itself.

It is the teaching methods that we employ and the extent to which we challenge and engage children that hold the key to the level of interest that teachers can generate and recreate on a regular basis. Implicitly, this necessitates that all children are working at a pace and level that is not only within their capabilities but genuinely stretches them.

The benefits of teaching lessons that children find stimulating are not confined to ensuring that a pleasant atmosphere prevails in the classroom and control problems are reduced. Children are more likely to remember information when they have received it in an imaginative and interesting way and, although 'interesting' and 'memorable' are two separate words, they cannot be divorced.

'Lessons should be hard to forget,' was the instant and authoritative reply of a Year 8 pupil to the prompt, *'What makes a good lesson?'* It is not only perceptive but crystallises everything that we as teachers are trying to achieve. Interesting lessons cannot be guaranteed to be memorable but are considerably more likely to achieve the aim of being hard to forget than lessons in which children have mentally switched off and are just going through the motions.

Who can *forget* the bucket of water that was thrown against the blackboard to simulate coastal erosion; the hosepipe that illustrated how electricity behaves in an electrical circuit; pulling the teacher's car to calculate force/weight ratio or recreating the trial of Charles I? Who can *remember* writing about the repeal of the Corn Laws or what the teacher had said about the latent heat of fusion?!

What questions did you ask today?

*'Millions saw the apple fall -
only Newton asked why.'*

B.M.Barach

When Einstein returned home from school his mother, or so the story goes, rather than asking him what he had done in school, always asked him, *'What questions did you ask today?'* It is a example we would do well to follow.

Asking questions is one of the most natural and effective ways of discovering new knowledge and deepening understanding yet, sadly, pupils spend very little time *asking* questions. *Answering* questions, yes, but I have already suggested in Section 2, relatively little is learnt by answering questions other than what is already known or not known.

Anyone who has spent any time around young children, either in the home environment or in infant school, cannot have failed to have noticed how many questions they ask. It is almost constant as lively, inquisitive minds explore everything around them. A barrage of 'What does that do? Why is that there?' can eventually try anyone's patience, but they are both learning and demonstrating a desire to learn that is as instinctive as it is insatiable. Contrast this with a typical secondary class; the questions have dried up, enquiring minds are no more and the quest for knowledge has all but ended.

Maybe I paint too bleak a picture but it is a scene that I have witnessed on many occasions and the more I see it the more concerned I become. I cannot help but wonder at the extent to which this process is inevitable or if the gradual reduction in a child's curiosity is somehow the result of the experiences they receive when they move on to secondary education. If this is so, it is unlikely to be the result of a conscious strategy - indeed many teachers would be horrified if they felt that their pupils were being restrained in this way. It is rather the product of many of the classroom strategies commonly employed in secondary schools.

My own experiences of secondary classrooms suggests that, while they are not actually discouraged from doing so, children are only rarely actively encouraged to ask questions. Asking questions to clarify what they are required to do or because they don't understand - maybe, but encouraged to ask questions because they are curious and wish to discover more, no. Worse still, the organisation and nature of many lessons can inhibit children, gradually stifling their natural curiosity to the extent that their innate desire to question that flourished during early childhood stagnates and eventually retards.

Yet should this be so surprising? At no time during my initial training or subsequent professional development was the significance of asking questions as part of the learning process stressed. Nor was I given guidance about how this important aspect of effective learning could be incorporated into my classroom practice. Judging by the large number of colleagues who I work with in Inset sessions who, while acknowledging the correlation between asking questions and effective learning, claim it had never really occurred to them before, my experiences are not uncommon.

Similarly this is not a notion emphasised by OFSTED. Certainly the old framework required inspectors to judge learning skills by such features as, *'A willingness to ask questions.'* while inspectors look for *'A willingness to ask and answer questions,'* as part of the new inspection process. However, this is hardly emphasising the fact that the learning process is enhanced by asking questions and teachers looking towards OFSTED for their guidance could be forgiven for failing to make the connection.

Yet despite giving less than clear guidance on this issue, OFSTED are critical, ironically so, of lessons in which children do not ask questions, claiming that learning is poor when pupils do not, *'Ask questions in order to develop their understanding of concepts.'*

The case for the defence of secondary teachers is further strengthened when the National Curriculum for Science is examined in close detail. As part of the programme of study, pupils should be given opportunities to : *'Ask questions, e.g. 'How?', 'Why?', 'What will happen if....?'*

As much as I am encouraged by this unambiguous guidance - although puzzled why this recognition of effective learning should be limited to the science orders - I am perplexed as to why this instruction should be limited to Key Stage 1, as by Key Stage 2 the order has been diluted to, *'Pupils should be given opportunities to ask questions related to their work in Science,'* and by Key Stage 3, the requirement for pupils to ask questions in order to enhance their learning, has disappeared all together!

The challenge for us as teachers is clear; somehow we have to change the emphasis of our lessons so that pupils spend more of their time asking questions rather than answering them. Pupils do not have to be taught how to ask questions - young children clearly demonstrate that this is instinctive - but they do have to be encouraged to do so. It is not always easy. We are battling against a number of years in which their natural desire to question has lain dormant, largely through no fault of their own. Our job is to rekindle their curiosity by providing them with opportunities that not only encourage questions to be asked, but positively demands them.

This has to be our conscious goal. Simply not discouraging them from asking questions is insufficient. We need to reverse a trend. We are battling against a lethargy induced by the early experiences of secondary schooling and consequently require an array of strategies, such as the ones suggested below, that we can call upon as and when appropriate.

Establish the atmosphere

Our first task must be not only to establish an atmosphere in which children feel that they can ask questions, but one in which they positively want to. It is as intangible as it is significant and the fact that it cannot be quantified does not mean that it is not instantly recognisable. It is not something that can be created as a one-off. Rather it must permeate all that we do in the classroom in a way that both reassures and inspires pupils to ask questions and learn on a daily basis.

Display the key questions

Display the key questions around the wall of your classroom, e.g.

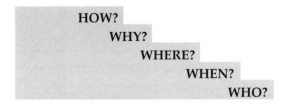

and refer to them whenever possible.

What questions did you ask today?

Use Einstein as your inspiration and display:

> *What questions did you ask today?*
> *(Einstein's mum)*

in a prominent place on your classroom wall.

As the pupils leave your classroom at the end of a lesson ask them *'What questions did you ask today?'* or get them to write them down. It doesn't have to be done at the end of every lesson but it can help to focus everyone's mind on the importance of asking questions if done on occasions. It is a strategy that can be employed by a subject teacher or by a form tutor equally successfully and can be particularly effective when followed up with, *'What did you learn today?'*

What would Einstein have said?

Is a question I often ask pupils at an appropriate stage in a lesson, to which they invariably reply *'Why is this happening?'* or a variation on this theme. It is a useful way of encouraging children to ask effective questions.

Ask questions yourself

Demonstrating that you yourself are prepared to ask questions is one of the most effective ways of creating the kind of atmosphere outlined earlier. Not only are you demonstrating a desire to learn and that nobody - not even experts - know everything, you are reinforcing the behaviour that you are encouraging your pupils to adopt, namely asking effective questions, in order to extend their knowledge and understanding. Children will quickly follow the example and it may well be that the teacher's curiosity will 'kick start' the pupils' dormant desire to question.

I recently observed a Year 8 Science lesson, in which pupils were giving a short report on the planet Mars that they had earlier researched for homework. One by one each pupil gave their report while the rest of the group dutifully sat and listened. At least, they sat in silence and looked to the front although whether they were listening - *actively listening* - I have to doubt, judging by the complete lack of reaction to any number of incredible pieces of information. As a non-specialist in Astronomy I was fascinated, learnt a great deal and was moved to say, *'Wow, I never knew that!'* on more than one occasion.

During the report on Mars, I was interested to discover that, *'There are polar ice caps on Mars and in the Summer they melt and in Winter they spread.'* I was naturally intrigued less than twenty seconds later when the report went on to say that *'...even on a summer's day the temperature never rises above freezing.'* The fact that no-one else in the room was similarly intrigued and moved to ask, *'How can ice possibly melt if the temperature never rises above freezing point?'* is indicative of the way the natural curiosity of many secondary school pupils has been suppressed. It also causes frustration and even sadness, but significantly little surprise.

It was left to me to express my amazement that ice could apparently melt without the temperature rising above freezing point and pose the question, *'How can this possibly happen?'* The fact that no-one knew the answer was nothing to worry about - the group all went away to try and find the answer, and indeed check the accuracy of the information, for homework - the cause for concern being that no-one asked the question in the first place!

Pupils have to ask a question

I discussed the lesson described above with the teacher concerned, who agreed to change the approach very slightly when repeating the lesson with a similar group a few days later.

On this occasion, pupils were required to identify one question that they wished to ask the reporter at the end of each report. To ensure that everyone was participating, pupils wrote their questions down and to eliminate the possibility of embarrassment, questions were plucked at random from a box.

The transformation was as obvious as it was dramatic - their body language was different, attention was written across their faces and they hung on every word, asking questions at every opportunity. *'What do you mean when you say the surface gravity of Mars is 0.38 x Earth's?'* asked one, *'What causes the dramatic drop in temperature on Mercury from around 430°c in the day to -180°c at night?'* asked another - something that passed by unnoticed days earlier-while virtually the entire class was eager to discover how ice could possibly melt on Mars when the temperature was below freezing!

This simple technique can be employed in many situations with equal effect: after a video, after reading a piece of text, after a demonstration etc. It is up to the teacher to select the appropriate time to introduce it.

Working in small groups

I recently observed a lesson during which the teacher paused and asked the class, *'What don't you understand?'* and gave them the opportunity to ask him anything they wanted. Nobody did. This was not because everybody had understood all the work, as was evident by the number of questions the teacher was later asked while the children attempted a piece of written work, but essentially because they were shy.

Many pupils are shy and live in fear of being laughed at or looking foolish if they get something wrong or admit to not understanding something. Consequently they don't - neither do many adults - and teachers who believe that all pupils would always ask in their classroom because of the atmosphere of trust that they had established are deluding themselves.

Although we should not confuse questions that seek to clarify what pupils are expected to do with questions that search for new knowledge and greater understanding, they cannot be entirely divorced in that both contribute towards learning and are arguably essential if learning is to be effective. If children are reluctant to ask questions in front of a whole class then we, as teachers, must accommodate their natural reticence by creating situations in which they are working in smaller groups. Pupils are far more likely to admit to gaps in understanding and ask questions if they are working with a few children that they get on particularly well with and trust.

Time-outs

Call a two minute time-out in a lesson during which pupils can talk to the people sitting next to them and ask them any questions they wish. Not only are pupils more likely to ask the questions they would be embarrassed to ask the teacher, they benefit from hearing explanations in their 'own language' while the child who gave the explanation will benefit from having to organise their thoughts in order to explain something to their friend.

Seeking help from a friend is something that we all did as pupils and something that pupils do in all classrooms, either in a whisper or when the teacher's attention is diverted - indeed it is the only way I managed to scrape through 'O' level Maths! It hurts no-one and benefits both parties, so why not make it a planned part of lessons? An additional benefit is that after talking together two pupils may identify a question that they wish to ask the teacher, something they may be prepared to do as a pair but would have been less likely to do as individuals.

What we are doing is formalising something that goes on in every classroom in the land, while drawing attention to the value of asking questions in order to seek clarification. Of course it is inappropriate when we are seeking to assess what individuals already know and can do but as a strategy to enhance learning and deepen understanding it is extremely effective.

Question wall/question box

Encourage pupils to either write questions on a specially designated area of the classroom - a question wall - or drop their questions in a question box. They can be anonymous to encourage shy pupils to ask questions, but need not be, and can be written up or dropped in at any time.

The advantages of encouraging pupils to highlight any questions that they wish to ask during, as opposed to at the end, of a unit of work or module are twofold. Firstly, any widespread difficulties in understanding or misconceptions are quickly identified enabling the teacher to take the necessary action and, secondly, aspects of the work that prove to be of particular interest to a significant number of pupils can be recognised and provide avenues for learning that would not previously have been explored. Although the scope for exploiting these tangential areas of interest are undoubtedly limited by the constraints of the National Curriculum, they need not be particularly extensive and can be dealt with in minutes or as an extra piece of research homework, for the entire class or individuals in it.

Ask the expert

It is possible to build into a task a requirement for the pupils to ask an 'expert' questions. The 'expert' is normally the teacher although this strategy can be even more effective when it is possible to arrange an alternative expert - a visitor or even another teacher who has some specialist knowledge - to be present.

For example, the news report task highlighted in Section 7, in which pupils are required to adopt the role of news reporters and investigate the earthquake that devastated Mexico City in 1985 includes the following opportunity:

You yourself know very little about earthquakes so you will have to do some research before you fly to Mexico. The editor has arranged for an expert to visit the office to give you some help. During his visit you may ask him any question that you wish. Please make sure that you have prepared some questions before his visit.

I have selected an example from a geography lesson although it is easy to see how this technique could be applicable in a wide range of subjects; a survivor of the Second World War in History, a religious leader in RE, an engineer in Technology, a microbiologist in Science, a leading local sportsman in PE or a native French speaker in Modern Languages.

It can of course be argued that the information that the pupils can glean from the 'expert' will be little, if any more, than they could have got from a text book or by being told by their teacher. While this may, in some instances, be true, this argument ignores the significant benefits of both rekindling pupils' natural tendency to ask questions so that once again it becomes habitual and the significant increase in motivation and attention that the approach undoubtedly brings.

Use the Internet

A number of questions that arise during '*Ask the Expert*' sessions lend themselves to the Internet. Demonstrating to children that no-one - not even experts (or teachers) - knows everything, is a healthy signal to give. We are all learning and by asking the right questions we can all extend our knowledge and deepen our understanding. In some respects answers to questions that the teacher does not know, or pretends not to know, can be more beneficial in that they can be used to initiate further research.

Answers can of course be found in a number of places including text books or asking another expert, but a spin-off benefit can be that pupils are encouraged to use Information Technology in the form of the Internet, which can often result in a further increase in motivation.

Some of the questions asked during the science lesson described earlier, for example:

'How can ice melt on Mars when the temperature never rises above freezing?'

'Why is the difference between the maximum and minimum temperature so great on Mercury?'

were successfully answered using the Internet.

Asking questions to provide a focus

One of my vivid recollections from primary school is sticking a teabag on a piece of paper and writing underneath it, *'This teabag comes from Ceylon.'* It was part of a project on Ceylon, now Sri Lanka, and something I frequently refer to as the 'Ceylon Factor'.

The 'Ceylon Factor' is when pupils include material in their projects, assignments or GCSE coursework that neither helps them learn - I already knew that tea was grown in Ceylon - or, in many cases, does not directly relate to the specific focus of the project. It occurs when pupils, lacking in research and independent learning skills, discover a resource vaguely related to the piece of work that they are doing and reproduce large sections, largely for the sake of it. It helps explain why teachers receive interesting but largely irrelevant information on Japanese customs, dress or diet as part of a piece of work on Japanese industry!

Identifying specific questions, such as , 'What are Japan's major industries?', 'Why is so much Japanese industry located around the coast?', 'Why has Japanese industry been so successful?' and 'How did Japan rebuild its industry after the Second World War?' at the beginning of the assignment clearly focus attention and investigation on the specific task in hand and is a way around the 'Ceylon Factor', particularly if the questions have been generated by the pupils themselves.

Differentiation by asking questions

There can be few teachers who are not aware of both the need for differentiation or of the possibilities available to them of differentiation by resource, task, pace, support and outcome. However, there will be fewer teachers who have considered the potential for differentiation offered by asking questions.

It is a technique that can be applied to a wide range of subjects and areas for study. In this instance it was used with a mixed ability year 9 group studying the European Union.

The European Union is an issue which for some reason seems to lend itself to rather undemanding and unimaginative learning tasks. Labelling the member states on an outline map of Europe and matching flags with countries is hardly intellectually challenging for pupils of average ability, never mind more able children, and yet both are activities I observe with alarming regularity.

The first step in this alternative approach is to discover what is already known about the issue, misconceptions and all, by asking the class to write down anything they know or have heard about the European Union. In my experience this is very little, although comments such as, 'It's where we all have to use the same money' or 'Isn't it somewhere in Brussels?' are not uncommon.

Having identified what is known and not known the next requirement is to establish what the group would like to, and feel they ought to, know. There are, of course, a number of ways this could be done, although I tend to favour asking individuals to write down the questions that they wish to know and briefly discuss them with their neighbour before bringing the whole class together.

It is at this stage that differentiation by asking questions becomes apparent as relatively straightforward questions such as 'Which countries are in the EU?' and 'When was it formed?' are compared with 'Does the EU achieve what it sets out to achieve?' and 'What is likely to happen to the EU in the future?' It is quite obvious that the nature and depth of the questions are directly proportional to the pupil's ability, as is their capability at researching the answers.

The questions form the basis of a groupwork assignment to produce a piece of work on the European Union. The groups contain a full spread of ability with all pupils given the task to research the answers that they are capable of. The more able are clearly motivated and appropriately challenged by the more difficult questions and do not have to waste time on, what would be for them, menial tasks, while the pupils of lesser ability do not have to struggle with concepts that are beyond them.

Encourage the pupils to ask the questions normally asked by the teacher

Picture a typical science laboratory: the teacher is demonstrating an experiment to a group of pupils and as the demonstration progresses asks questions designed to help the pupils make sense of the proceedings. This strategy - a combination of questions and explanation - is extensively employed by teachers and by no means confined to science lessons. Inevitably, the pupils, however able and well motivated, are reliant, arguably over-reliant upon the teacher to ask pertinent questions at the appropriate time. If children are to develop into autonomous and effective learners our challenge must be to develop their ability to ask the relevant questions independently.

As teachers all we need to do is to stop asking the questions and encourage the children to ask them instead. While few teachers would not welcome the prospect of their pupils interrupting lessons with *'Why is this happening?'* or *'What would happen if you used a different chemical?'* most would be rightly sceptical of whether children so used to observing and responding to prompts from the teacher could immediately switch role and become the initiator of such perceptive and incisive questions.

Their scepticism would be well founded and the shift in role needs to be done gradually. All that is required to begin this process is for the teacher to pause at the appropriate moment in the experiment and say, *'I would normally ask a question at this point - what do you think I would have asked?'* Children will very quickly grasp the idea and the need for the teacher to prompt questions will dramatically reduce.

Asking questions as a basis for taking notes

Secondary pupils are usually ineffective note takers, largely because few are ever taught this difficult but important skill. The ability to take notes is dependent on the identification of key points and therefore central to effective learning. It is also fundamental to a person's ability to learn independently while at school and after they have left.

Children should be taught how to take notes, not in isolation but as part of a genuine learning experience, and one of the most effective ways of developing this skill is by asking questions. Give the pupils a piece of text such as the one found overleaf. In this case it is about hurricanes, but before you let them read it ask them what they wish to find out from it. If they are new to working in this way they may need some help to identify relevant questions but they will soon get the hang of it.

Questions such as *'What are they?'* and *'In what part of the world do they occur?'* immediately spring to mind and are arranged across the page as follows:

What are they?	Where do they occur?	Can they be predicted?	What causes them?

The text is then read a sentence at a time. If the sentence answers one of the questions that have been identified the information is noted in the appropriate column. If it doesn't, there is no need to write it down.

Hurricanes are violent storms consisting of strong winds, dense cloud and torrential rain. The winds blow in a circle and can exceed 155 miles per hour although the centre of the storm, known as the eye, is usually strangely calm.

Hurricanes are also known as Typhoons and Cyclones and occur around the equator in an area of the world known as 'The Tropics'. Once formed they move in a curved path at a rate of anything up to 50 miles per hour.

They always begin to form over an ocean and are caused by warm, wet air being pushed upwards by denser, colder air.....

What are they?	Where do they occur?	Can they be predicted?	What causes them?
Violent storms Cloud, rain, strong winds (up to 155 miles per hour) Blow in circle	Around the equator (Tropics)		Warm, wet air is pushed upwards by cool, dense air

These strategies are of course not exhaustive. Nor do I advocate them necessarily being adopted wholesale. They are, however, practical suggestions, variations on a theme, that can be adapted to meet the particular requirements of any subject area or set of circumstances. They are not more time consuming, nor do teachers risk losing control; they are simply effective classroom strategies and approaches that bring immeasurable gains in both motivation and learning.

They acknowledge the need for secondary school teachers to do more than not discourage pupils from asking questions and recognise that our challenge is to actively recapture the spirit of curiosity that is so tragically diluted, or worse still lost, around the time that the children transfer to secondary school.

Activities like these must not be employed as 'one-offs'. Asking questions can both develop and satisfy a thirst for knowledge and understanding and our challenge is to create and maintain an atmosphere in which asking questions is the norm.
This atmosphere must permeate and underpin everything we do in the classroom and the fact that it is intangible does not lessen its importance.

We must not be discouraged when children demonstrate a reticence to ask questions when introducing these strategies for the first time. I have known painful silences and blank pieces of paper when asking children for the first time what they wish to discover about a particular issue. Far from being a surprise we should be expecting this response from pupils who have quickly grown accustomed to their passive role in formal education. Reversing this habit is a gradual process and one that requires a great deal of patience and no little skill.

Far from being a chore we should view this as an essential investment, an investment that, given time and perseverance, will yield a rich harvest of curiosity and effective learning. Done well, we are doing more than stirring a dormant instinct by encouraging children to ask questions. By prompting them to ask the right questions at the appropriate time we are developing an autonomy essential if lifelong learning is to become a reality.

> *Once you have learned to ask questions - relevant and appropriate and substantial - you have learned how to learn and no-one can keep you from learning whatever it is you need to know*

Postman and Weingartner
'Teaching as a subversive activity.'

Section Six

'Thinking is so important'   Edmund Blackadder

Edmund Blackadder had it right; thinking **is** important. This particular Blackadder pearl of wisdom was inspired by Baldrick's reluctance to express an opinion and respond to his master's enquiry about what he thought about a particular painting. You may remember the scene: after several unsuccessful attempts to elicit Baldrick's thoughts an exasperated Blackadder was reduced to clipping his servant around the ear while muttering in unmistakable Blackadder style, *'Oh Baldrick, thinking is so important!'*

And so it is. It both underpins and drives the learning process and as such is a pre-requisite of effective learning and genuine understanding. For learning, thinking and understanding are inextricably linked; genuine long term learning requires understanding. Without it, information is nothing more than a temporary visitor to our short term memory. Learning without understanding is superficial - indeed , it is doubtful if we can claim to have learnt something if we do not understand it. Similarly if we understand something it is far easier to learn and far more likely to find its way into our long-term memory. While in-depth thinking about an issue does not guarantee that we will understand and learn it, it greatly enhances our chances.

Consider the things that you find or have found difficult to learn. It is likely that these are also the concepts that you have struggled to understand. For understanding is the key to effective learning and, in turn, thinking is the gateway to understanding. In many respects the oft quoted Chinese proverb which ends, *'I do and I understand'* would be equally valid if it ended, *'I **think** and I understand.'*

It would appear that Blackadder and I are not alone in holding thinking in such esteem. The National Commission on Education certainly does, claiming that *'effective learning requires the development of thinking skills,'* and arguing that good teaching will encourage children to, *'think for themselves.'* So too, does Sir Ron Dearing who contends that children ought to, *'think things out for themselves,'* while OFSTED include, *'challenge their thinking'* as one of the new criteria for judging effective lessons. Indeed there can be few educationalists who would not endorse the pivotal role that thinking plays in the learning process with even Her Majesty's Chief Inspector acknowledging that children achieve more when teachers *'challenge their thinking.'*

There is equal agreement that a key part of effective teaching is to develop understanding. In the original OFSTED Framework, Inspectors were required to judge the extent to which teaching strategies were appropriate to *'ensure that pupils develop understanding,'* while the revised guidance acknowledges that teachers should, *'challenge pupils and deepen their knowledge **and** understanding.'* The umbilical link between thinking and understanding is also recognised by OFSTED, who contend that, *'where practice is effective—interaction between staff and children is used to extend thinking and understanding.'*

Whether this will be the outcome if children spend vast amounts of time listening to the teacher or writing notes is however extremely doubtful and, while every teacher will have their own tale to tell, there is more than a suspicion that there are a great many lessons in which thinking is conspicuous only by its absence. That is certainly the conclusion that one is tempted to draw from the scattergraph in Section two and helps explain why so few children readily associate thinking with lessons.

Stretching the minds of young people does not happen by chance but as a result of carefully designed activities and a conscious strategy. Listening and writing notes, while effective techniques for transferring information, are not such activities and are less than conducive to extending thinking and understanding. All too often it appears we allow ourselves to be deceived by something that masquerades as thinking, confusing low level tasks with genuine cognitive activity.

Judging by the frequent references to a general lack of challenge and the need to generate more thought and understanding in lessons made in a succession of OFSTED subject summary reports, this is more than a personal view. The following quotes are taken from a range of subject reports between 1992 and 1995:

- *'Insufficient attention continued to be paid to —- the development of understanding.'*

- *'The pupils were not required to take initiative or think for themselves.'*

- *'The pupil's had a good knowledge —- but their levels of understanding were much more variable.'*

- *'Where learning was less effective they received and produced information without fully understanding it and were, therefore, unlikely to retain it.'*

- *'Written tasks gave the pupils few opportunities to develop their understanding in any depth.'*

- *'Too much direction from teachers in some schools restricted the ability of pupils to think sufficiently for themselves.'*

- *'Poor standards were reported —- where copying of work (and colouring in worksheets) resulted in no proper understanding.'*

- *'There is a tendency in too many classes to 'spoon-feed' rather than to encourage students to think ideas through for themselves '*

- *'Learning that is over-directed by the teacher or by worksheets often produces only superficial knowledge without real understanding.'*

- *'The range of teaching approaches should be reviewed to ensure that pupils are appropriately challenged to think for themselves.'*

OFSTED are right. Reviewing our range of teaching approaches is exactly what we need to do. The extent to which children are being challenged to think and helped to understand is directly related to the nature of the activity they are involved in. We are not searching for separate activities. The relationship between thinking and understanding is such that activities which challenge children to think in depth about an issue will almost certainly contribute to enhanced understanding.

Developing understanding.

I once overheard a year 10 pupil express her delight that she was to be taught by a particular maths teacher. When I asked her why she was so pleased, she replied that she had always found maths easier to understand when she had been in his class. She found it harder to tell me why she seemed to understand things better with the teacher concerned, but when pushed for an answer gave the following 3 reasons:

i)   he simplified things
ii) he was prepared to go over new material as many times as necessary
iii) she felt she was able to ask him questions and admit when she didn't fully understand something.

Simplifying things.

The extent to which children understand difficult concepts is directly proportional to the teacher's ability to simplify the concept to a level that they can cope with. In many respects the ability to simplify even the most difficult concept is the very essence of teaching and a quality which to a very great extent is inherent.

Repeat things.

Good teachers will repeat things as often as they need to before a child fully grasps a new idea. This is no great problem in the unlikely event of all the children in a class struggling to grasp the same point, but presents the teacher with a considerable dilemma if only a small minority of the group are having difficulty. On these occasions the teacher must not only give the struggling pupils the extra explanations they require but ensure that the rest of the children are not held back. This can only be done if there are occasions when the teacher frees him/herself from the responsibilities of whole class teaching in order to give children the personal attention they deserve. (Strategies for doing this are explored in more depth in Section 7.)

Create a climate which encourages children to ask questions.

All teachers exhort children to ask for help when they don't understand. Despite the fact that many teachers genuinely encourage pupils to ask for help when they need it and are more than sympathetic when responding to such requests, many children are reluctant to admit to gaps in their understanding. It is human nature, and even those teachers who skilfully manage to create and maintain an atmosphere of trust and mutual respect, still face the problem that many children are reluctant to request help.

While these feelings are not erased, they are significantly reduced if the child does not face the ordeal of seeking help in front of the whole class. Again, the key is to provide children with sufficient personal attention in order to give them an opportunity to ask their questions in relative privacy. Indeed the teacher need not wait for the child to admit to having difficulties. It is often possible to detect which children are struggling with their work and if a class is well known to a teacher it is often possible to predict with considerable accuracy which children are likely to struggle with particular tasks and which children will be reluctant to ask for help. Talking to individuals or small groups gives the additional advantage of allowing the teacher to explain a difficult concept in a manner and in a language that is particularly appropriate to the individual or individuals concerned.

How do you know if they've understood something?

Understanding is a double-edged sword. Not only do teachers have to develop understanding in young people, they also have to gauge how successful they have been. The example in Section 2 illustrates how difficult this is. The vast majority of children would have correctly answered that the Mexico City earthquake was caused by movement along the subduction zone but the teacher would have had no way of knowing how many pupils, if any, understood exactly what a subduction zone was.

Consider this example, which comes from a Year 8 science lesson. The children are answering questions from a text book. An extract of the text reads—

> *Humus is found in the soil and is mostly made up of dead plant material which is slowly rotting. It helps to keep the soil in good condition - for one thing it breaks down to give chemicals which help plants grow.*

The questions inevitably include:

Q) What is Humus?
Q) Why is it important?

Many of the answers, not surprisingly, are remarkably similar and read something along the lines of —

A) Humus is mostly made up of dead plant material which is slowly rotting.
A) Humus is important because it helps to keep the soil in good condition It does this by breaking down to give chemicals which help plants grow.

Almost without exception the children got the questions correct, received their ticks and words of encouragement and the teacher entered the marks into the mark book. Superficially, at least, it had been a successful lesson. Talking to the children individually after the lesson however, it was clear that, although the majority of the class had indeed understood what humus is and why it is important, around eight children, despite answering the questions successfully, had virtually no idea what this stuff called humus was or what it did.

Sadly, this is in no way uncommon and comes as no surprise if the nature of the activity is closely analysed. Not only does it fail to develop understanding to any significant depth, the nature of the questions enable them to be answered without any significant appreciation of what humus is and therefore leaves the teacher with no indication how much a child has understood. It rather begs the question what was the objective of the lesson, or more specifically the activity? If it was to challenge thinking in order to develop the pupils' understanding of humus, it was ineffective. If it was to assess who had understood what humus is, it was inappropriate.

An alternative way of using the same piece of text in order to challenge pupils to think about humus, develop their understanding of it and gauge the extent of that understanding, would be to set the following task—

Q) Explain what soil would be like without humus. Give reasons for your answer.
Q) Can you think of anything else that is like humus?

It takes no longer than the questions it replaced, required no further preparation and would be suitable for children to complete individually or in pairs. While the group work, the teacher is free to give children the individual attention and help they need if they are to develop their understanding to the depth they are capable of.

Change the form of information.
There is little value in giving children a graph for them to draw or asking them to copy a diagram. Again, these activities do little to develop understanding and do not enable the teacher to assess what has been understood. Instead, adopt the principle that all information has to be changed into a different form, in order to challenge thinking, develop understanding and obtain a clear indication of what has been understood.

Thus children can be asked to turn a piece of text into a diagram, describe what is being shown on a graph, or explain a particular issue using a diagram as a prompt.

Relate difficult new concepts to familiar experiences.
Children find it easier to understand the process by which water vapour rises on convection currents, cools and condenses back into water droplets when watching steam rising from a boiling kettle only to turn into water droplets upon hitting the ceiling.

Similarly, the difficult-to-grasp notion of invisible electricity travelling around a circuit, is made rather easier when children are simultaneously watching water circulate around a coil of hosepipe, the impact of switches and the behaviour of a bulb being simulated by the water tap and a simple fountain.

Children teach each other.
Many teachers would agree that they learnt more about their subject when they started teaching than they ever did during their formal education. In order to teach it is first necessary to be absolutely clear about what you are trying to say and organise your own thoughts to an extent that is not required when simply learning something. These benefits are equally applicable to children and asking pupils to teach each other represents a very effective teaching strategy. The fine details do not matter - the activity can be conducted in pairs, small groups or a children can address the whole class - it is the principle that is important.

What would you tell your ten year old brother?
Teachers are often reluctant to adopt strategies such as pupils teaching each other because they fear an increase in the noise level and a possible breakdown in discipline. However the principle of pupils being placed in the role of teacher need not be done at the expense of control.

Invent a fictitious 10 year old brother or sister for each member of the group who on the child's return home enquires what their elder brother or sister has done in school that day. Whatever the reply, be it rotational symmetry, exfoliation or Hookes Law, the younger child asks. 'What's that then?'

It is an activity that is equally suitable for home or class work and can be a written or verbal exercise. Teachers can learn a great deal about the extent of a child's understanding simply by listening to the explanation they would give to their imaginary relative. They can also make the situation a little more realistic by throwing in the inevitable *'why?'* and *'how?'* in the appropriate places!

Earlier I suggested that one way of increasing understanding is to simplify the issue in question. Normally this is done by the teacher for the benefit of the pupil. In this instance however it is the pupil who has to do the simplifying in order to explain something to somebody who is a couple of years younger. This process can only be beneficial as by simplifying something for themselves they are essentially making sense out of a concept in a way that means something to them.

It need not be a lengthy exercise, nor is it one that need be adopted every week, but as an exercise to make children think, develop their understanding and allow the teacher to assess the extent of their understanding, it is extremely effective.

Explain how to do something.

After children have been introduced to a new skill, such as how to do simultaneous equations and have spent all lesson practising, ask them to write down a step-by-step guide to the technique in order to think about and reinforce what they have learnt. It is of course an variation of the strategy outlined above and again is equally effective as a verbal or written exercise.

In whatever guise it is something that we don't ask children to do often enough. It is much more usual for the teacher to provide an explanation of how something is done and ask the pupils to write it down. While this may guarantee the correct information finding its way into every child's book for future revision purposes, it does little to deepen a child's understanding and makes it impossible to detect those children who have misunderstood.

See something.

It is far easier to understand something if you have seen it or seen it happen and it is the reason why field work and educational visits can be so effective. If it is not possible for children to see what they are studying first hand then show them a video. If there is no video, show them a photograph or give them a demonstration.

Do the same thing in a different way.

Covering the same learning point in a variety of ways - video, written exercise, oral work - is beneficial, arguably essential, for two reasons. The likelihood of children understanding something if it has been reinforced on a second and even third occasion is significantly greater than if has just been covered once, but the real benefit is in catering for the needs of children with vastly different preferred learning styles.

Individual children learn best in different ways: some learn effectively reading from text while others require a more visual approach to learning as provided by a video or a demonstration. If we do not vary the way in which we teach we are disadvantaging children whose preferred learning style is significantly different from our usual teaching approach.

Strategies to encourage children to think

Despite its importance, thinking has something of an elusive quality; rather like the wind we cannot see it, only the evidence of it. It is difficult to define and harder to measure and yet, in the same way that a parent knows if a child is sleeping or merely pretending, a teacher instinctively knows when a pupil is deep in thought. It is unmistakable and the fact that it is so hard to pin down does not reduce its significance in any way.

It should not be regarded as a bonus when children are deep in thought, but as a pre requisite of effective lessons. As such it must both pervade and underpin everything that we do in the classroom and determine the activities that we adopt and the way in which we teach. We must create an atmosphere in which thinking is positively encouraged and considered the norm - rather than the one-off occasions that the young boy I overheard saying *'Oh this is one of those lessons where we have to think,'* when he discovered his science lesson was to be a CASE session (Cognitive Acceleration in Science) obviously experiences.

It will not happen by chance but as a result of a conscious strategy and activities that are specifically designed to stretch the minds of young people. The following activities do precisely that. So too do many of the activities described earlier in this chapter and throughout the book. Given that they are all designed to challenge children's thinking, many are inevitably variations on a theme. They are not by any means exhaustive and can be adapted to suit the requirements of the particular circumstances.

What is the most important word?

The class is an intermediate Year 10, the subject Science. The teacher is asking who can remember the diagram of the Nitrogen Cycle which the group had copied last lesson sufficiently well to draw it on the board. No one can. Eventually the pupils are allowed to refer to their notes and someone is press-ganged into drawing the diagram. It is all very ordinary with few thinking beyond the very lowest level.

Next door a similar group cover the same topic. After an initial explanation, the teacher gives the group 2 minutes to write down the answer to 2 questions; *'Which do you think is the most important word in the diagram?'* and *'Why?'* They work in silence, doubtless encouraged by the fact they cannot get either question wrong, their faces revealing the difficulty in selecting just one word.

Subsequent discussion and a show of hands revealed strong support for the word *nitrogen* while a few had selected *cycle* with a lone girl settling for *bacteria*. The various factions attempted to justify their selections, the argument that the whole thing was about nitrogen being countered by the 'cycle supporters' who maintained that the key point was its cyclical nature while a lone voice remained adamant that it was bacteria that drove the entire process and without it the Nitrogen Cycle would not exist.

The discussion continued unabated until the bell brought proceedings to an end, a final show of hands revealing a number of pupils who had changed their mind during the discussion. The entire exercise had lasted less than 15 minutes but judging by the response at the start of the next lesson to the question *'What is the Nitrogen Cycle?'* the benefits had been way out of proportion to the time spent on it. It was far from ordinary.

Asking pupils to pick out key words or sentences can be an extremely effective task that is simple to organise, does not need to be time consuming but focuses children's attention and requires them to think. It is also an activity that can be arranged in many different ways.

What is the most important sentence?
All teachers are well aware that when a group of pupils are asked to read anything only a very few will actually read it properly. At best children will read uncritically without really thinking about the message of the text. At worst they will look in the general direction of the page.

To focus their thinking simply ask them to pick out the most important sentence and be ready to justify their choice. Do this and you have a very different lesson. Of as much interest as the sentence they choose is the reason for their choice - it tells the teacher much about their level of understanding.

Six key words
Consider the following paragraph:

> Onion skin weathering or exfoliation is a type of weathering commonly found in deserts. During the day the sun heats up the rock causing it to expand but at night it becomes cold and the rock contracts. Continual expansion and contraction gradually weakens the rock until eventually bits break or peel off like the skin of an onion.

A typical way of using this information would be to ask questions such as; *What is exfoliation? Where does it take place?* and *What causes it?*

As we have already seen in a number of examples, it is possible for a great many children to answer questions like these with apparent success, even though their understanding of the particular issue may be extremely limited.

An alternative way of using the text would be to challenge pupils to identify the 6 words they consider to be the most important in a given amount of time. (The number of words will depend on the nature of the text, but should ensure that the pupils are faced with a dilemma.)

This activity is equally effective with individuals working in silence or for pairs or small groups to discuss the problem but at some point the class needs to be brought together so that the words that have been selected can be written on the board. If the text has been well chosen there will almost certainly be more than 6 words nominated, leaving the class with the task of reducing the list to the required number. Each word can be considered in turn with the child or children who nominated it being asked to justify its inclusion. In many respects, this is the most valuable part of the exercise.

As the debate unfolds it becomes apparent that particular words are important for different reasons and are actually the answers to a variety of questions. *Desert*, for example, tells us where exfoliation takes place. Other words such as *peel* describe what is happening, while there are words like *contract* that explain why the process takes place.

It is not difficult to link this exercise with the principle of children asking questions as part of the learning process, outlined in Section five. It can be interesting to speculate which question Einstein would have asked - *where is it happening? what is happening?* or *why is it happening?* - if he was a pupil in the class. There is always almost universal agreement that Einstein would have been eager to identify the main reason for the process and would therefore have almost certainly asked, *'Why is this happening?'* - although one pupil thought Einstein would have asked *'Why are we limited to one question?'*

By the end of the lesson, pupils will have an excellent understanding of the process of exfoliation and will quite happily explain exactly what it is and why it occurs. Many people, pupils and teachers alike are absolutely amazed when they realise that at no point during the lesson did the teacher tell the class anything about the process and that their understanding has developed as an exclusive consequence of being challenged to think.

If you are sceptical try it for yourself. Pick out your 6 most important words, justify them to yourself and then try to select the single most significant word from your short list. If you are already familiar with the process of exfoliation simply choose a different piece of text.

It should also be pointed out that there is a huge spin off benefit from working in this way. Identifying and recording key words or key points is the very essence of effective note taking and therefore lessons like these provide excellent opportunities for introducing and developing this skill, which is so fundamental if children are to develop any autonomy as learners. At the end of the exercise children will be left with 6 words such as; *desert, hot, expand, cold, contract, peel, gradually, continual,* on which to base their homework.

Impose a limit
One of the problems that teachers frequently face is receiving work of considerable volume but lacking in understanding. This is particularly common when pupils have been involved in research or project work and tends to be particularly acute when Information Technology in the form of **'Encarta'** or something similar has been used to obtain information.

Imposing a limit is a way of encouraging children to use resources a little more critically by forcing them to think carefully about which pieces of information they can afford to leave out, a process that simultaneously helps them to identify the key points while developing their understanding.

For example, children may be given a 100 word limit and asked to summarise a project or extended piece of work. Alternatively they may adopt the role of a news reporter and be given a 30 second slot to report back to the class. The report is prepared for homework or in a previous lesson and pupils take turns to respond to the news readers prompt—— *'Figures released today reveal Japan as one of the leading industrial nations in the world. We have sent our industrial correspondent to Tokyo to find out why.'*

It is an exercise that not only requires children to consider the issue in some depth, but also develops their confidence and ability to speak in public.

5 Key words / 1 word
Extend the principle of reducing information down to the key points and conclude a piece of work by identifying the 5 or even 1 key word(s).

In the example outlined above, the group had been studying Japan and her industrial strength as part of a module on Industry. From the outset they were aware that they would be required to identify the 5 words that they thought best summed up Japan. Having selected their words each pupil compared their list to the person sitting next to them, focusing their attention on the words that appeared in only one of the lists.

Having discussed the likely words with a partner, pupils took it in turns to read out a new word until all the words considered important had been read out, giving a final list of: *successful, crowded, mountainous, rich, volcanic, islands, vulnerable, prosperous, hi-tech, industrial, inventive, technological, skilled, educated, innovative, loyal and industrious.*
To round off the exercise pupils use their chosen 5 words to construct an individual acrostic poem.

Thus a 2 week project has been summarised in 100 words or a 30 second news report which has in turn been condensed into 5 key words that are easily memorable in the form of an acrostic poem. Not only therefore has information been passed through the brain on 4 separate occasions, it is virtually impossible to complete steps 2 and 3 - summarising the project in a news report and identifying the key words - *without* thinking. Go on, try it!

Sequencing.
Take a paragraph of purposely written text. For example:

> The sun is virtually overhead at the equator all year round. The sun heats up the earth. Any moisture on the earth's surface is evaporated. The water turns into invisible water vapour. The water vapour rises on hot air currents. Hot air currents are called convection currents. As the air rises it cools. Eventually it cools so much that condensation takes place. Condensation is when invisible water vapour turns into water droplets. The droplets are light enough to 'float' in the sky as clouds. As the droplets touch each other they join together and get heavier. Eventually they get too heavy and fall to the ground as heavy rain. This is known as convectional rain.

i)   Cut the text up and jumble up the order of the sentences.
ii)   Sit pupils in a line at the front of the room, facing the rest of the class. Give each child one sentence.
iii)   Each child in turn reads out their sentence. The paragraph will not make very much sense.
iv)   The group can then make suggestions to re-arrange the order of the sentences so that the paragraph makes sense. e.g. *'The sentence about condensation needs to come nearer the end'* or *'Duncan should be sitting by Rachel.'*
v)   The paragraph is then read out again. The process is repeated. Each time the text should make a little more sense, until finally the correct order has been established.

An exercise like this will take around 30 minutes. By the end of it children may not know every thing there is to know about convectional rainfall and will certainly require the teacher to go over the process, adding some detail, but they will have begun to think in some detail about what is happening, with the very process of placing the events in the correct sequence helping to develop their understanding.

Borrowing an idea from Section five the pupils can be given an opportunity to ask a question once the sequence has been established - *why does hot air rise? why does air cool as it rises?* - in order to deepen their understanding still further.

Sequencing is a strategy that can be adapted and effective in a range of subjects, including history, geography and science. Less obvious is the potential for using this technique to develop an understanding of poetry or the order in which calculations are done when solving equations.

Prediction.
Predicting the outcome or possible outcome of an event or the implication of a change in circumstances is a particularly effective way of challenging children to think - we often include the phrase *'What do you think?'* in the question. Again predication is a strategy that is suitable in a wide variety of subjects.

WHAT

would happen if you changed it for a negative number?

do you think would have happened if the USA had not entered the second world war?

would happen if the temperature drops by 2 degrees?

do you think would have happened if Scott had taken 4 men, not 5 to the pole?

will happen if the current is reversed?

In a similar vein, read out the first sentence or paragraph of a story and ask children to write the last line. Alternatively give them 3 possible story outlines and ask them to which the opening sentence belongs. It simply cannot be done without thinking - have a go!

Do the 3 hardest sums.
We are aiming to create an atmosphere where thinking is encouraged and accepted as the norm. To that end it is important that we utilise every opportunity to encourage children to think.

Instead of giving out a worksheet and informing the group that it contains some questions or calculations that, while on the same topic, are more difficult, warn the class that you are about to give out some harder questions and ask them to predict what they will be like. Alternatively, issue the questions and ask why they are more difficult.

On the same theme, give out a sheet of questions or calculations and ask each child to do the 3 that they consider the most difficult. As they complete their task - which cannot be completed without a great deal of thought - wander around the class and ask children what influenced their choice. Their answers will tell you a great deal about their level of understanding.

All of the strategies outlined have one thing in common; they are conciously designed to make children think. These approaches, really they are variations of one approach, challenge children and involve them in their learning to a far greater extent than many of the alternative strategies described in Section 2. There are, of course, no guarantees, but they are based on the premise that by engaging children in thought, and actively developing understanding, all children will leave their lessons with a much greater chance of having *learnt* something.

'The needs of the one outweigh the needs of the many.'

Captain James Kirk.

In much the same way that Spock was left on a distant planet to die, sacrificed so that the Enterprise and her crew might be saved because, *'The needs of the many outweigh the needs of the one'*, the interests of individual children are often sacrificed in order to satisfy the needs of the majority of their class.

Mine certainly were in the maths and geography lessons I describe in Section 4 and I suspect that there are many teachers who would admit, if only to themselves, that there are children in at least some of their classes who regularly find the work soaring far above their heads while a handful of pupils coast along relatively unchallenged. Even for those teachers who cannot relate to the Star Trek analogy, the picture of the classroom will be instantly recognisable.

OFSTED, while telling us that a key factor in successful teaching is, *'matching work to the pupil's different and developing abilities'*, also report that, *'there is poor match to the developing and different abilities of pupils in about a quarter of schools.'*

While this is maybe a little misleading - it is far more likely that all schools possess some teachers or departments who fail to match work to different abilities as effectively as they might while under the same roof there are colleagues who have considerably more success - it does give us some indication that a gap exists between what is generally accepted to be good practice, and what is going on in classrooms up and down the country.

This view is confirmed by the reference to the lack of differentiation and the need to cater for differing abilities more effectively in the vast majority of the OFSTED subject summary reports between 1992 and 1995 including - English, maths, science, modern languages, geography, history, technology and music. They paint a bleak picture.

OFSTED reports, both school and subject summaries, are littered with comments such as:

- *'Lessons were rarely planned to take account of the abilities of individual pupils.'*

- *'There was little evidence of work differentiated according to ability.'*

- *'Too little attention is given to matching the work closely enough to the ability of the pupils.'*

- *'There was a general lack of attention to differentiation.'*

- *'The greatest weakness in the planning and therefore the execution of lessons is that individual needs are inadequately considered.'*

- *'Lack of effective matching of tasks to the ability of pupils remained a persistent problem.'*

to such an extent that suggests differentiation is an issue for a great many schools, departments and individuals. Ask any cross-section of teachers to identify the three things about their job that they find the most difficult and it is hard to imagine that any single issue would be nominated as frequently as catering for pupils of different ability in the same class.

It is fully accepted that these observations, in effect they are criticisms, are susceptible to the weaknesses inherent in any generalisation, and it is important to acknowledge that there are notable exceptions of both individual teachers and departments who are effectively catering for different abilities on a regular basis. By definition, however, these exceptions are in the minority and matching work to children of different ability remains an issue that as a nation we would do well to address.

However, differentiation is difficult. As a teacher the odds are stacked against us and no one should pretend otherwise. Many teachers go to extraordinary lengths and give up a considerable amount of their own time to try and cater for individual needs, but maybe it is inevitable that in most classes a small number of pupils will find the work beyond them while one or two may find most things a little easy. It is certainly tempting to think so. Maybe we should be satisfied with meeting the needs of most of the group most of the time.

Captain Kirk wouldn't be, I am sure of that. Indeed he wasn't. Against all the odds he returned to eventually save the previously abandoned Spock, because to Kirk at least, *'The needs of the one outweigh the needs of the many.'* It is this sentiment, that should be the motto of all teachers, that justified not only Kirk's enormous effort for what was after all just one member of his crew, but justifies the time and effort that teachers all need to make if children, however few are not to be abandoned on far away fictitious but symbolic planets, their only crime that they are different from the majority in their class.

Few, if any, would dissent from Captain Kirk's view that the needs of all children deserve to be met. Teachers do not need OFSTED to remind them that not only is learning extended when all children are able to work at an appropriate level but, for both ends of the learning spectrum, gains in academic achievement are frequently accompanied by enhanced motivation and the reduction of behavioural problems. Kirk, it would appear knew a thing or two about teaching as, from whichever angle the issue is viewed, accommodating the needs of the one can only be regarded as an essential ingredient in the effective classroom practice recipe.

Many would argue that catering for individual needs is made easier when pupils are placed in groups according to their ability. Providing that the groups are not fixed for more than one subject, this strategy can indeed reduce the problem of coping with vastly different needs and bring potential gains, at least in purely academic terms. The caveat here is that grouping pupils by ability is seen as a substitute for differentiation when clearly it is not. OFSTED recognise this danger and remind us that: *'Where setting is used too much can be taken for granted about the homogeneity of the group.'* and that, *'Whatever form of pupil grouping is used, it is essential that teachers plan for the full range of ability within each class.'*

Differentiation is a challenge that cannot be side stepped by simply arranging pupils in ability groups as all groups contain both a range of ability and individual needs. Many would argue that the size of the challenge is directly proportional to the range of ability. This maybe so, and I am not attempting to argue the case for one method of grouping children over another, but simply emphasising that whatever the size of the challenge it can only be met successfully by adopting teaching strategies that will enable all the children in the group to flourish and achieve what they are capable of achieving.

In many respects the acknowledgement that individuals should be given every opportunity to achieve their full potential has been, or at least appears to have been, central to many of the educational reforms of the last ten years. That is certainly the conclusion that must be drawn from the then DFE's claim that an *'emphasis on the needs of the individual child'* is one of the *'fundamental principles which run through all our policies.'* This is entirely consistent with the objective of the National Curriculum, as stated in all of the original subject orders, namely to *'ensure that each pupil should obtain maximum benefit, by offering pupils the opportunity to reach the highest possible achievements.'*

Kirk would not be alone in applauding the philosophy, but it is a goal that will not be achieved simply by statutory requirements. It is not the National Curriculum that will enable young people to fulfil their potential, or at least narrow the existing gap between potential and achievement, but the way in which the orders are interpreted and delivered in the classroom. It has always been so. Long before the educational reforms of recent years good teachers were aware, acutely so, that the children in their class had varying amounts of ability and potential. The National Curriculum did not give birth to differentiation, but simply placed it in the spotlight.

Since its arrival in the spotlight we seem to have discussed very little else - even if the results of our effort's have been somewhat variable - and no matter which school you teach in or your subject specialism, differentiation has been one of **the** words of the nineties. It did not exist when I started teaching, in what was admittedly a very different world although actually not that long ago, but has emerged as one of the most used words of its generation in such a manner that I feel almost guilty that I cannot remember, as people remember the Kennedy assassination, where I was when I first heard it.

Certainly you would be hard pushed to find a School Development Plan that doesn't include reference to it and if you haven't recently been on a course titled 'Effective Differentiation in — (insert the name of your subject here), then you have every right to feel aggrieved because virtually every other teacher in the country has. Coupled with a plethora of books and pamphlets on the issue that have flooded the education market and appear in all staff libraries - between the publications about daily collective worship and school development planning in practice - it is not surprising that we all at least know what differentiation is.

Consequently, the obligatory differentiation question is answered without undue difficulty at interview, candidates almost without exception happy to both confirm their personal commitment to the value of differentiating their lessons and to reveal a range of strategies that they can adopt in order to do this. Differentiation by resource, task, pace, support, and even exposition roll off the tongue in much the same way as the Geological Time Scale rolled off mine - Pre Cambrian, Cambrian, Ordovician - the day after I had spent all night memorising it in preparation for the morning's 'O' level paper.

The concern lies not in the quality of the interview answers but that the strategies, so easy to outline, are often conspicuous by their absence after the candidate has been appointed. The irony of the situation while inevitably frustrating is not, or certainly shouldn't be, surprising for they are sadly absent from a great many classrooms.

Yet why should this be so? In recent years we have talked about it, read about it, been on courses about it and devoted more time and energy to it than arguably any other single issue. Some however remain wary of it, others daunted by it while some regard it as part and parcel of classroom life. To some it comes naturally, some have to work at it, while others ignore it altogether.

The reasons for this are twofold: firstly, we have become guilty of talking too much about differentiation to the extent that all we have succeeded in doing is overcomplicating the issue, almost regarding it as something we do in addition to teaching. It has developed an elusive, almost mystic quality and, like some beautiful apparition, has become something that appears all too infrequently, fading away just before it can be grasped. It has a tendency to appear in some classrooms more regularly than others, while its occasional appearance in some classrooms has gone undetected.

Despite all the hype, differentiation is, in essence, all about adopting the teaching strategies that will enable individuals within a group to flourish. There is no substitute for it, no wonder book or worksheet than can be distributed among the class, no secret way of organising the furniture in your room that will miraculously enable all children to achieve, no differentiation equivalent of the Blarney Stone. Deep down we all know this yet still teachers go on courses looking for quick fix, off the peg solutions, returning disappointed because there are none.

Secondly, it is apparent that differentiation is not something that just happens, it has to be planned for, and this is particularly true if children of differing abilities are going to be given different resources or asked to undertake a variety of tasks. Planning in this detail inevitably takes an enormous amount of time and competes with a multitude of other commitments and demands, and there can be little blame attached to individual teachers who, after teaching a full timetable, attending the inevitable meeting and completing the day's marking, do not always have the inclination, never mind the energy, to start preparing differentiated work for the next day.

It is for this reason that individuals working in isolation, even with the very best of intentions, will make relatively little impact and necessitates a concerted and departmental approach to tackling differentiation. In Section 8, I suggest that departmental meeting time should be devoted largely to developing and improving classroom practice, taking the yardstick that teachers should come out of a meeting potentially a better teacher. There is no issue more central to improving classroom practice than preparing lessons that are effectively differentiated and yet it is something that appears on departmental agendas infrequently at best.

The following strategies have proved to be an effective way for departments to develop differentiation.

- Collectively and individually review your current approach to differentiation. Which strategies do you currently adopt? Which prove particularly successful? What existing barriers do you face when trying to differentiate your work? - the way pupils are grouped, the layout of the classrooms, curriculum organisation, existing resources etc.

☞ Section 8 on developing classroom practice is appropriate for any teacher or department wishing to develop strategies for catering for the needs of individual children. In particular, what can you learn from observing your colleagues in action?

☞ Spend departmental meeting time planning lessons that take into the account the needs of individual children. (Ban any other agenda item for a year and see what a difference it makes to your teaching!)

☞ Where possible, lessons should be planned by a minimum of a pair of teachers, or preferably in threes. The norm in this country is for teachers to plan their own lessons, even when the teacher next door is covering exactly the same material with another group. One teacher plans the core activities while a colleague prepares work for the for the slower learners and the more able children. Planning should involve both the selection of suitable resources and the preparation of appropriate tasks.

☞ This principle should be extended and teams of three be responsible for writing schemes of work, which can also be prepared in meeting time. All schemes of work should be written at three levels: core, extension and less able.

☞ A storage and retrieval system should be adopted for teachers to share the work that has been prepared.

☞ It may be more appropriate to hold a weekly meeting of 30 minutes rather than hold a 90 minute meeting every third week.

☞ Only those members who are teaching the particular topic being prepared need attend the meeting.

☞ Review the way in which pupils are grouped in your department. Although I have stressed that it is important to differentiate work even when children are grouped by ability, the nature of individual subjects may lend itself to a particular form of grouping. Are the needs of all children best met under your present system?

☞ Review the current procedure for in-class support. (This may also need to be done at whole school level.) Is the most efficient use made of human resources? Explore ways in which in-class support could be extended - would members of the department be willing to give up a non-contact period to support a member of staff or children who had been identified as needing particular attention? It need not be weekly commitment, once a fortnight or half termly would be an improvement on the support that children currently get. Staff are more likely to do this if at least some of the jobs that they do during free periods are being done at the new look departmental meetings! Alternatively, it may be possible to trade the sacrifice of a free period for a guaranteed non-contact period at another time in the week. However it is arranged, schools and departments who are seriously committed to raising the level of classroom performance would do well to make every effort to increase their provision of in-class support.

There is, however only so much that can be done before the lesson and although it is unlikely that the needs of individual children will be met without adequate preparation, planning alone will not ensure that differentiation will take place.

Much depends upon the teacher, both on their selection of suitable teaching strategies and on their ability to implement them effectively. For differentiation is more than a worksheet or variety of resources; the very essence of differentiation is acknowledging that some children will need things explaining more than once while others will be able to work at a faster pace and be able to understand the material to a greater depth. Substitute the phrase 'personal attention' for the word differentiation and the mists that have shrouded, and for many obscured, the issue suddenly lift.

Personal help and individual attention is something that all children require on a regular basis. It is a time when explanations can be given as often, as slowly and as simply as necessary and questions can be asked to clarify misunderstandings. Not only is it necessary if learning is to be as effective as possible for all members of a group, it is something that learners of all ages crave, as anyone who has ever observed teachers during an IT INSET session would testify.

Take any child that you teach and spend just ten minutes on three separate occasions talking to them about their work, answering their questions and explaining things in a way and a language that they understand and notice the significant improvement in both their work and attitude. Unfortunately, many of the classroom strategies that are frequently employed by secondary teachers do not allow the teacher the freedom to do this as they are almost continually engaged in teaching the whole class and it is significant, to me at least, that not one child has ever responded with *'talking to the teacher'* in the word association activity referred to in Section 2.

If you are sceptical of this claim refer to your scattergraph on page 18 and consider how the learning activities that you frequently employ allow you to talk in any detail with individuals on anything like a regular basis. Better still, keep a record of every time you talk to a child about their progress or an aspect of their work that goes beyond giving them a correct spelling or a reminder to underline the title.

If the lack of contact with individual pupils alarms you, you are not alone. In 1993 a survey conducted for the National Commission on Education revealed that a staggering 44% of pupils in Year 7 had never spoken to their class teacher about their work, while the corresponding figure for Year 9 was 45%. When we meet with individuals so infrequently, it is little wonder that individual needs are so rarely met.

Our challenge as teachers is to create sufficient time during lessons to provide the personal attention that all children need if they are going to make the progress they are capable of. We must, on occasions at least, free ourselves from the constraints of whole class teaching, and think less of 9A and more of Benjamin, Sarah and James.

This is not a comment on the merits of whole class teaching. There is no doubt that used selectively and executed by a lively, enthusiastic teacher it can be an effective and stimulating learning experience. However, if we accept that individual children have significantly different needs, then we must also accept that those needs cannot be met if they are all doing the same thing all of the time. It was Thomas Jefferson who said, *'There is nothing so unequal as to treat unequal children equally.'* and he was right.

If the key to effective differentiation is providing children with the help and support that they require then the focus of our attention must be on the strategies that will release the teacher from whole class responsibilities. These fall into two categories and are particularly effective when employed in tandem. Our first task is to identify ways of releasing teachers from dealing with much of the trivia that characterise so many lessons and, secondly, we need to develop tasks that do not require the constant supervision of the teacher.

Getting rid of the trivia.

The prime role of a teacher must be to teach. The excessive amount of time therefore when we are dealing with relatively trivial matters can only be regarded as a waste of time because if we are dealing with trivia, we are prevented from helping children learn. In many lessons we are reduced to a cross between walking dictionaries and professional 'fetchers' of anything ranging from scissors to new exercise books - the extent to which we help anybody learn being confined to making sure they have the correct page and know what the title is.

Keep a count, or ask a colleague to keep count of the amount of 'housekeeping' questions you answer in a typical lesson.
Better still keep a stopwatch on the amount of time you spend responding to children's basic needs and compare it to the amount of time you spend sitting down with children in order to help them learn. You will be horrified!

Employ a resource trolley.

In order to prevent the constant barrage of requests for resources, keep all the resources that could possibly be needed for a lesson - scissors, paper, glue etc. on a trolley or in a box and get them out at the beginning of every lesson. They do not have to be on a trolley- the principle is one of open access - but it can be an advantage to lock resources in a storeroom at the end of lessons and at break and this is easily and quickly done if they are mobile. It may take a lesson or two for children to get used to the idea but they soon will, leaving the teacher free to get on with the central business of lesson - learning!

Develop independent learning skills.

This does not mean that children should be able to teach themselves, but simply work independently on occasions without having to constantly seek help from the teacher and they will only be able to do this if they have previously been taught some basic skills. In many respects it is an investment. They do not necessarily require high order skills to enable them to work alone for significant periods but if all children could use a dictionary, a contents page and an index the frequency with which they needed to interrupt the teacher would be vastly reduced.

Look at it from another angle; as the teacher - freed from whole class responsibility- would be sitting down with another child discussing their work, the more problems such as finding correct spellings that children can solve for themselves, the less frequently they need to interrupt a fellow **pupil** and deny them some of the help and attention they deserve.

Develop tasks to free the teacher

Although it is important that teachers do not spend lessons fetching resources and dealing with low level enquiries to the exclusion of helping children learn, the introduction of a resource trolley and the development of basic study skills alone, will not provide teachers with the time they require to help all the children in a group make the progress they are capable of. This will only be achieved if teacher led, whole class activities are replaced on occasions by individual or group tasks.

The specific nature and organisation of these tasks is unimportant. What is crucial however is the principle:

> **Engage children in a task so that the teacher can be released to provide the individual help and attention that all children require if they are to flourish.**

Differentiation should not be faceless. It has, or should have, a soul. It is not about tasks and resources - it is about people, or more specifically about personalising learning. All children need to be helped, to be stretched, to be corrected, to be reassured, to be encouraged, just to be noted - it is the very essence of differentiation. Tasks are not our goal - differentiation by task can be cold and isolating - simply the means to enable us treat classes of 30 or more as individuals.

That is not to say that the quality and nature of the tasks are unimportant, simply not our prime motive. Yet we must not lose sight of the fact that they are learning experiences in their own right and as such we must ensure that they are equally worthwhile and effective as the whole class activities that they replace.

The caveat exists however that when teacher-led whole class lessons are replaced wholesale with a succession of low level comprehension or 'fill in the missing word' type worksheets, the quality of learning will deteriorate. The fact that pupils of different abilities are given different worksheets that use a different vocabulary may mean that the lesson is differentiated and may enable children to complete the tasks but often this is done without developing understanding or promoting genuine learning. It is almost differentiation for the sake of it and when this happens there is a very real danger that our attempts to meet the needs of the one are made at the expense of the many.

Tasks come in all shapes and sizes; some may last as little as 20 minutes or a lesson while others will last for a week or longer. Some will be for individuals while others will be for pairs or small groups. On occasions all children will be given a common task, alternatively the children could be set different tasks that are variations on the same theme. The whole group may work from the same resource while at times it will be more appropriate to issue a variety of resources of differing difficulty. It matters not. Whatever the combination of task and resources:

the principle remains the same and it is the individual support that is the crucial factor.

Short and extended tasks

Any task that does not involve the teacher addressing the entire group at the same time offers an opportunity to provide individual support. Clearly, however, the longer the activity will last - and here lies the real benefit of extended tasks - the greater the opportunity to work with individuals and small groups.

When tasks are too short, teachers are reduced to dashing around the classroom offering help in a manner akin to a cabaret perfomer spinning plates. Not only is it tiring to the extent that teachers are understandably tempted not to bother trying, it is also relatively ineffective as inevitably there is only time to talk to a handful of children. As some children, notably those with some degree of learning difficulties, demand a large proportion of the teacher's time and teachers rightly 'spin the less able plates first', some children - usually the quiet pupils in the 'middle' of the group - never get seen.

The teacher has the choice, either invest in some roller skates or extend the length of the task.

Extended tasks

The task overleaf is an example of just such an extended task: Not only does it provide extensive opportunities for the teacher to work with individuals, it is a worthwhile learning activity in its own right and incorporates many of the factors that contribute to effective learning.

Referring to it as a task is a little misleading - as part of the project, children will be involved in some research, they will listen to the teacher, have the opportunity to ask questions, interrogate text, decide what to include in their report, draw maps and diagrams, and watch videos, in order to gain enough knowledge and understanding to enable them to write a report that both describes and explains the events surrounding the earthquake in Mexico City. That amounts to more than a task and would be more accurately described as a series of learning experiences encompassed within the overall end product of a news report.

The main features include:

Resources

Children are not confined to the resources provided by the teacher and they can be encouraged to search for additional material in books, magazines, CD Rom or on the Internet. The resources that are provided are suitable for a range of ability, the teacher having ample opportunities to guide pupils to the most suitable resource.

Asking questions

Building in an opportunity for children to identify the questions that they wish to ask an expert is a strategy described in Section 5 and is a feature of effective learning. It is not a requirement of all tasks, but one that can considerably enhance the learning experience. In this instance it represents an effective introductory activity; children have to begin thinking about the issue in some depth and identify both what they already know about the topic and what they need to know. Asking questions about any issue, in this instance children might well ask, *'What are earthquakes?' 'What causes them?'* and *'Why was there an earthquake in Mexico city?'*, not only stimulates curiosity but is the very foundation of independent learning.

Teacher exposition

The alternative would be for the class to be briefed by an expert - the teacher - before they 'fly out to Mexico'. In other words the teacher would conduct a whole class session to outline the key features of earthquakes and possibly ask a few questions to encourage the pupils to think carefully about some of the issues.

This clearly demonstrates that tasks like these should not be confused with teaching strategies that require children to simply discover things for themselves, although an element of guided research can be extremely effective, as they can include what may be regarded as traditional whole class activities involving the teacher in the role of subject expert instructing the class. The key difference here however is that this activity is part of a wider strategy that includes the opportunity for the teacher to work intensively with individuals and small groups.

Assignment - Earthquake!

You are a news reporter and this is your lastest assignment.

It is September 1985 and news is just coming in of a massive earthquake in Mexico City. Your task is to investigate this incident and write a **major** news report.

The report should include the following information:

- What happened during the Mexico City earthquake.

- Why the earthquake occured.

- General background information about earthquakes. (Assume your readers know nothing about earthquakes - you will therefore need to explain any technical terms)

Research

You yourself know very little about earthquakes so you will have to do some research. Your editor has kindly arranged for an expert to visit your office to give you some help and answer any questions you may have. He will be visiting for one hour on .... Please make sure that you have thought about the questions that you wish to ask before his visit.

Other places to find information include;

Interactions - **D. Waugh**
People in the Physical Landscape - **N. Punnet**
Earthquakes, Volcanoes and Mountains - **T. Crisp**
Physical Geography in Diagrams - **R. Bunnet**
Physical World CD ROM (editor has access)
Encarta (editor has access)

Deadline: Your report MUST be on the editor's desk by ....

There is a place for teachers addressing the entire group at the same time and is often a suitable strategy to launch an extended task. However the range of ability present in any group, but particularly in mixed ability classes, will limit the effectiveness of any such explanation, restricting them to a general, introductory outline. The opportunity for in-depth teacher instruction, pitched at exactly the right level for the individual or group concerned comes when the class have embarked on their task and the teachers whole class responsibilities have been lifted.

Providing children with individual attention and support

As soon as the children begin working on their task the teacher is free and the quality of the learning experience and the extent to which individual needs, not to mention potential, is met, depends to a very great extent on how the teacher uses this freedom. It is not a time to catch up with reports, but a golden opportunity to help children learn. Helping children learn, whether they be extremely able pupils or have significant learning difficulties, is not something that presents teachers with too much difficulty. The difficulty, arguably the impossibility is trying to cope with children at either end of the spectrum simultaneously. In this way they don't have too.

The way in which the support for individual children is organised is unimportant and teachers, having taken into account the nature of the task, the particular mix of children and the layout of the room, will all have their own preferences. Children can be seen individually or, if appropriate, in small groups. The teacher can move around the room or the pupils can move to the teacher. It doesn't matter. What matters is that children have an opportunity to talk to the teacher about their work.

The dialogue between teacher and pupil will have a different focus, depending on the stage of the task. Loosely, these discussions fall into three categories although elements of all three categories may well be present each time a teacher talks to a child.

Early on the teacher will want to spend time with children **clarifying** and helping them **plan** their response to the task. At this stage the teacher will also want to check that the child has chosen to use resources appropriate to their ability, if a variety of resources are available. It can be beneficial to talk to less able children first in order to make sure that they are clear about what they are being asked to do.

At some stage during the task the teacher will want to talk to children about the content of their work - in other words teach them! The key benefit here is that **explanations** can be given in a language and at a level that is appropriate for the child or group of children and not pitched to the middle of the whole class. Able children need stretching and deserve explanations that go deeper than many children of their age group can cope with. They also need the opportunity to ask questions and explore issues at tangents. Similarly, more modest attainers often need things explaining more than once. For these children explanations need to be slower, simplified and given in less technical language. In many respects children learn more in 5 minutes of intensive tuition than they do in 5 lessons working at a level that is inappropriate to their ability.

There are two more significant benefits from 'teaching' children in small groups that are often overlooked. Firstly, it is far less likely for attention to wander- something that can happen when even the most inspirational teacher whole class teaches for longer than a few minutes - when the teacher can maintain almost constant eye contact with the entire group and when the significantly reduced numbers involved allows far more interaction between teacher and those being taught than is possible with a complete class. Secondly, children are far more likely to admit to gaps in their understanding and to enter into dialogue with the teacher if they do not have to do so in front of the entire class. Some children go for weeks without talking during lessons and, while children who are naturally shy do not become outgoing overnight, they are much more likely to converse with the teacher if they can do so individually or in a small group with children they trust and feel comfortable with.

During their discussions, teachers will have an opportunity to **assess** each child's level of understanding and the quality of their work. Assessment is more than just marking books and is so much more effective when carried out face to face. When whole class teaching teachers simply do not have the opportunity to talk to children about the things they are doing well and things they need to improve. Communication is often limited to the comments that teachers write on pieces of work although these are seldom read and even more rarely digested as they compete in vain for attention with the mark on the bottom of the page. Not only is the assessment process more effective when conducted in person, it is not confined to the end of a piece of work when it is often too late to do anything about it. It is easy for a teacher to assess a pupil's level of understanding and identify at an early stage misunderstandings that the child can rectify, providing teacher and child have the chance to talk to each other while the child works.

The strategy I describe is not differentiation by task, by resource or by outcome. If you are desperate for a label, and I am not, it might most accurately be described as differentiation by support. I would rather not call it anything however. It is quite simply effective teaching as it provides children with the individual attention that is required for effective learning.

Although I shy away from labels and jargon, I am aware that the strategy that I have outlined is closely related to Supported Self Study and Flexible Learning. In these approaches - really they are a single approach under different umbrellas - extended tasks may be summarised in 'study guides' and giving children individual help and attention may be referred to as *'tutorials'* or *'academic tutoring'*, but, whatever it is called, the principle of releasing the teacher from constant whole class responsibility in order that they can help individuals learn remains the same.

So too, do the benefits. In *'Flexible Learning:Evidence Examined'* (**Network Educational Press, 1993**) I outlined the key findings of a four year research project that used a range of techniques to examine the impact of teaching in this way - using study guides to outline extended tasks in order to free the teacher to support children on an individual basis - upon the academic attainment of over 120 pupils.

The results were dramatic. Not only did the children unanimously report that they enjoyed working in this way - necessary if learning is to be effective - but there also were significant learning gains across the entire range of ability.

What else are meetings for?

I started this book by drawing attention to Chris Woodhead's plea for teaching to be placed high on the agenda for discussion, It is a sentiment I wholeheartedly concur with, yet sadly I doubt whether it appears on the agenda, never mind enjoys a prominent position on it, for the majority of teachers and the majority of schools. Yet, ironically OFSTED report that the quality of teaching is an issue identified in 50% of school inspections.

As a profession we spend many hours in meetings and talk about a great many things. Some are worthwhile, many clearly are not. Somehow it seems we manage to find time to discuss whether children should be allowed to wear overcoats in corridors or eat in their form room but never seem to get around to discussing really important issues such as how children learn or effective teaching strategies. It is a situation that will not be unfamiliar to a great many teachers, many of whom I suspect will share my frustration.

Reflect on the meetings you have attended, or ran, this term and consider how many of the agenda items were really necessary and how many of them helped those attending the meeting to become more effective at their job. Yet I know of few teachers who do not wish to develop their expertise or who are not prepared to spend long hours to provide a better quality of experience for their pupils. Equally I know of few teachers who do not resent wasting their time discussing relative trivia.

Teachers should come out of meetings potentially better teachers - if this is not the case then don't have them. Of course it will be necessary to consider administrative matters on occasions to ensure that the department runs smoothly but these should be kept to a minimum to allow meetings to be devoted to developing teachers and improving the quality of their teaching. An effective way of dealing with much of the inevitable routine administration is to produce a weekly or half termly departmental newsletter or develop a system of communication via a departmental notice board which allows the focus of departmental meetings to be events in the classroom.

At the very least start or end each meeting with a good idea for a lesson or invite members of the department in turn to describe a strategy or activity that has proved to be particularly successful. Better still, create a culture of reflection and continuing professional development and give the clear message that there can be nothing as important for teachers than to consider what goes on in classrooms. We can all develop and improve our practice, from the newly qualified young teacher fresh from ripping up their metaphorical L plates to the most experienced campaigner who has been teaching longer than they care to remember. Similarly, it is criminal to allow all the experience and expertise of older teachers to go to waste without finding a way of passing some of it on to the next generation.

We cannot expect teachers to improve by chance, nor can we rely on professional development to be an inevitable by-product of experience. Professional development is both an entitlement and a necessity if the quality of classroom experience is to continue to improve and as such should not be *ad hoc* but a deliberate, structured and supportive process that underpins the drive for school improvement. A suggested approach is outlined below. It challenges teachers to think about and reflect on their current practice and it is the process of reflection, observation and development that is the key to developing further effective practice.

A central message of this book has been that it is insufficient, not to mention futile, for politicians to simply exhort teachers to become better practitioners. Before anyone can improve and develop they have to know exactly what they are aiming for and this is becoming increasingly unclear as a result of the confusing and often contradictory messages emanating from central government.

It helps explain why a young colleague who was raving about how brilliant a lesson he had just observed, was unable to explain precisely why he thought it to be so effective or what he could do differently in the classroom to improve the quality of his own teaching as a result.

Define effective practice.
An effective starting point for developing practice is to challenge teachers in an Inset session or departmental meeting to identify characteristics of a good lesson or, more specifically, a good science or maths lesson. I sometimes ask teachers to imagine that they have been asked to write the OFSTED criteria for the quality of teaching from scratch or that they have been asked *'What makes a good science lesson?'* by a student teacher. There are of course many ways of organising a session like this although it may prove effective to ask people to consider the matter individually before the group shares its ideas.

Identify the key features of effective practice.
To focus thinking even further, and in keeping with many of the effective learning strategies outlined in this book, challenge the group, individually and collectively, to pick out the key factor that makes a lesson effective. An alternative is to provide a list of criteria and ask people to place them in a rank order of importance or select the 3 key statements. The inevitable discussion that this activity generates is a particularly effective way of focusing attention on classroom practice and forcing teachers to consider the issue in some depth. It is something that we as teachers do all too rarely - not because we don't consider it important but because we simply don't have time. Changing the focus and style of the traditional departmental meeting not only gives us that time but ensures that our thinking is firmly on lessons and learning.

Refer to the OFSTED criteria.
Compare the list that has been generated with the OFSTED criteria for effective teaching. Many teachers are both surprised and reassured that the two lists are, usually at least, very similar, with factors such as: thorough planning, suitable resources, a variety of activities and children being motivated and on task, invariably identified.

Highlight the importance of learning.
I have argued in this book that lessons should be all about learning and have suggested that there are numerous examples of lessons which, while meeting many of the criteria of effective lessons, as identified by both OFSTED and the majority of teachers, actually contribute relatively little to helping children learn.

Few teachers, unless they have read this book, explicitly identify the promotion of learning as a key indicator of effective practice and it can stimulate further thought by challenging teachers to complete the sentence, *'Children learn effectively when —-'* An alternative but equally effective stimulus for reflection and discussion is the prompt, *'Children fail to learn effectively when —-'*

Agree what makes a good lesson.
It may be beneficial at this stage to allow the group to reconsider their criteria for effective lessons, taking into account the OFSTED criteria and the results of the *'Children learn effectively when—'* exercise. The ultimate aim is for the department or group of teachers to agree on what makes a good lesson.

Stick a reminder to your desk.
Sitting around a table discussing classroom practice is something of a luxury and features of high quality teaching that seemed so obvious during an Inset session are easily forgotten during the hurly burly of school life. In Section three I outlined what I consider to be the five key facets of effective learning and these, along with the questions, ***'How is this helping them learn?'*** and ***'What have they learnt?'*** are stuck to my desk as a constant reminder.

Reflect on your own practice.
Having agreed what constitutes effective teaching the next step must surely be to establish to what extent it is taking place in your lessons or in the department as a whole. The very process of debating what constitutes effective practice, trying to establish the relative importance of these features and considering the conditions that are required for genuine learning to take place, will inevitably have encouraged teachers to reflect on their own practice.

This needs to be extended and formalised with teachers being encouraged to go away and compare the way in which they are performing in the classroom with the criteria that they themselves have agreed constitute effective practice. This is essentially a form of self-evaluation and as such a non-threatening exercise, particularly as there is no compulsion to make their conclusions public. Teachers are not being judged by inspectors or other teachers, simply measuring their effectiveness against their own agreed criteria. Some of the questions posed in this book and the scattergraph exercise outlined in Section two are a useful starting points for self-reflection.

Be observed.
The process of establishing how teachers are currently performing in the classroom is made even more effective if the individual concerned is willing to be observed by a colleague, and essential if a teacher is to establish a clear picture of what is taking place in their classroom. Feedback, initially at least, should be factual as opposed to judgmental, the aim being to give the teacher being observed an accurate picture of what took place during the lesson. For example the observer may report that the introduction lasted 17 minutes or that a total of 11 questions were asked, of which 8 had been directed to boys. Try this exercise yourself and you will be amazed at the difference between your perception of events during a lesson and what actually happened.

The choice of observer is crucial: it need not be a more experienced member of staff, simply a colleague that the teacher trusts and does not feel threatened by. This feeling is strengthened if the pair are acting in the role of observer for each other. Eventually it may be agreed that the observation and feedback will focus on one particular aspect of the lesson such as how the teacher stretched the most able or the amount and type of questions that were asked.

Receive feedback.

While feedback that is essentially factual is helpful for teachers as they reflect on their own classroom performance, in order for them to significantly develop their practice it may be necessary to extend the nature of the feedback eventually to include an element of judgement. Giving such feedback requires considerable skill and no little sensitivity but when done well can be a positive and worthwhile exercise that both encourages and enables teachers to develop. Equally receiving feedback that is insensitive or unduly negative can result in teachers feeling threatened and becoming defensive with the chance of any subsequent development remote. Rather like teaching there is no right way of giving feedback but the following points may prove a useful guide, particularly for people with little experience.

- ☞ Always start by highlighting the good aspects of the lesson.

- ☞ Find out what the teacher thought of the lesson. Questions such as *'Which aspects of the lesson were you particularly pleased with?'* and *'Which parts of lesson do you think you could have improved?'* can be useful starting points for discussion.

- ☞ Try and reach a consensus view of the lesson. When you have witnessed an ineffective lesson try asking the teacher to identify an alternative way of approaching the lesson and then discuss the advantages and disadvantages of the two approaches.

- ☞ Ask the questions *'What did they learn?'* and *'How do you know?'* and consider the answers together.

- ☞ Relate the lesson to the aims and objectives. To what extent were they achieved? How do you know?

- ☞ However poor a lesson has been, only highlight one aspect of the teacher's performance that could be improved. Not only is it more effective to deal with one aspect of classroom practice at a time, it is counterproductive to demotivate a teacher by overwhelming them with a range of issues that they need to address. The teacher who has been made to feel inadequate is less likely to want to develop.

- ☞ Base all your observations on evidence.

- ☞ It is imperative to offer constructive advice about how the teacher can improve and develop. Offer the teacher the chance to observe you, or an accomplished colleague, implement the suggestions that you have made.

- ☞ Agree a target or a lesson when the teacher can try out your suggestions. Offer to observe and/or support

Observe other teachers.

Observing other teachers is, quite simply, the single most effective way of developing your own practice. The more you see, the more ideas you get and the more chance you have of witnessing different styles and strategies. Observation need not be confined to teachers of the same subject - as a geography teacher I learnt more about groupwork from a particularly effective linguist than any geographer - it is the methodology not the content that is of interest. In any school there will be outstanding teachers, many of whom will have a particular strength such as differentiation or groupwork. How sad that so few of their colleagues are given the opportunity to observe and learn from them.

Any school or department committed to improving the quality of teaching can make no more worthwhile investment than to ensure that all teachers are given the opportunity to observe colleagues, particularly effective colleagues in action. Like many good ideas in education however we never quite get around to it, mainly because we are so busy surviving on a daily basis. However, if we seriously want to become better teachers we have to make it happen. Go on, arrange to observe a colleague tomorrow!

Plan lessons with other teachers from your department.
We don't do this because we don't have time, but if departmental meetings were spent planning lessons then there is no such excuse. Discussing the most effective way of helping children learn a particular aspect of your subject and hearing how other teachers would approach the lesson can only be beneficial, particularly for teachers with relatively little experience.

Plan a lesson with a teacher from another department.
Although there is obvious value in working within a department, planing lessons with teachers from another subject area, at least on occasions, can be equally beneficial. Not only do they bring a different perspective and experience of alternative teaching strategies, they are non specialists and are therefore in an ideal position to pose the question, *'How will this activity help me **learn?'***

Walk before you can run.
Do not attempt to drastically alter your approach to teaching overnight. Develop one aspect of your classroom practice and do not attempt to develop another until you are comfortable with the new techniques. Too many changes at the same time can lead to chaos and de-motivation. There is no need to change your approach with all your teaching groups simultaneously. Choose the group that you have the best relationship with and you are most confident with to introduce new activities and only adopt them wholesale when they become second nature.

Don't try and teach old dogs new tricks.
By the time children reach Year 9 they have grown accustomed to a particular classroom experience and have become set in their ways Attempting to teach them in a significantly different way can lead to resentment and unnecessary difficulties. Introduce any significant developments in your practice to young children so that they grow up with the approach and accept it as the norm.

Inherit a group.
When trying strategies for the first time it can be advantageous to work with children who are used to working in the particular style that you wish to adopt. Without making it obvious to children it can be possible to inherit a class at the beginning of the year who have been used to the strategies that you intend to adopt with another teacher in order to make your task that much easier.

Teach another subject.

Almost by definition we find our own subject easy - it is almost second nature. Try teaching a subject that you yourself find difficult. It will force you to think carefully about concepts that you, and in all probability the children, struggle with and your inevitable and involuntary reaction will be to simplify whatever you have to teach. Compare your approach in this 'foreign' subject with the way in which you teach your own and see if there are any lessons to be learned.

Work as a department.

In Section seven I suggested that teachers trying to cope with the challenge of differentiation made relatively little impact when working in isolation. This is true of any initiative. Teachers who are trying to develop their classroom practice in isolation face a difficult task and are unlikely to make significant progress. The mutual support and encouragement that occurs when departments work together can lead to significant developments and can be a positive and rewarding experience.

Include suggested teaching strategies on all schemes of work.

OFSTED tell us that this increasingly the case in many schools. This is encouraging news and will do much to help teachers develop their practice. The strategies that are suggested on the scheme of work can provide teachers with some welcome guidance, but it is the process of deciding which strategies to include that is particularly significant. Schemes of work should not be written by individuals but by teachers working and discussing in pairs and groups and anyone tempted to say *'Ah but there isn't time'*, knows the answer!

Devote meeting time to developing classroom practice.

Spend meeting time reflecting on classroom practice, planning lessons and preparing resources. Ban all other items from departmental agendas and see what a difference it makes to your classroom practice. At the very least start each meeting with a good idea for a lesson or an outline of an activity that has proved to be particularly successful - after all, what else are meetings for?

Section Nine

'Ah, but...'

Inevitably there will be 'Ah, buts': *'Ah, but if you teach like that you will lose control,'* and *'Ah, but you can't teach like that and cover the National Curriculum,'* are two of the most common, but virtually anything can follow 'Ah, but...' if you really want it to.

Control, understandably, is a major concern of a great many teachers and most of us would admit to a feeling somewhere between unease and panic when a colleague, particularly a senior member of staff enters our room when the class is being noisy. Silence equates with effective practice in the eyes of many and we all feel the need to prove ourselves to our colleagues.

Even the most inexperienced teacher is acutely aware that their choice of activity contributes significantly to the atmosphere in the classroom and that certain types of lessons are recipes for potential mayhem, while alternative strategies contribute in no small way to an orderly lesson. Not only are we all aware of these strategies, we have all used them on occasions during our career - and no doubt remember with affection the groups that we were forced to use them with - simply to survive.

That itself is not a problem. The fundamental importance of maintaining an orderly classroom - it is a prerequisite for effective learning - should not be underestimated. Nor should the difficulty of establishing such conditions with particular children. However, there must be concern when the relentless struggle for control becomes a preoccupation and is achieved at the expense of providing children with genuine opportunities to learn. This situation can easily arise if the strategies that contribute to maintaining order in the classroom are confused with those that enable children to learn effectively. Let us be honest with ourselves when we adopt a particular technique; asking a potentially rowdy class to copy off the board on a Friday afternoon is designed to keep them quiet, not help them learn.

Many teachers are, of course, well aware that these less than challenging tasks contribute very little to a child's understanding, but adopt them anyway, simply to allay their anxiety of losing control - their perceived dichotomy being that they equate activities that they readily acknowledge help children learn with the potential for noise and disruption. Yet controlling a class is not our ultimate goal. It may be our first objective but should be regarded as no more than a platform to promote effective learning rather than be as an end in itself.

We must also find a way of balancing the need to cover an exam syllabus or Programmes of Study with the necessity of challenging children's thinking in order to develop their understanding. The National Curriculum, even post-Dearing, is content laden in all subjects and the prospect of covering it in its entirety is daunting to say the least. Consequently schemes of work now allow only one or two lessons to cover what previous generations of teachers would have taken weeks to teach. This pressure is compounded by the atmosphere of accountability brought about by SATs and published league tables which ensure that schools, departments and individual teachers are under the microscope like never before.

There is little doubt that a combination of these factors has had a significant influence upon classroom practice as many teachers have adapted their teaching to both ensure coverage of a crowded statutory curriculum and to prepare pupils for the demands of public examination. For many this has been a deliberate response while for others an involuntary reaction to the enormous pressure they face. Either way the consequence is the same as many of the strategies that develop understanding and help children learn are abandoned on the grounds that they are too time consuming, only to be replaced with activities which while efficient in terms of curriculum coverage, are less than challenging.

'Ah, buts' must not stand in our way. Whether they be excuses to hide behind or genuine concerns they must not be allowed to deny children the experiences they need if they are to develop their full potential as learners. In many respects they have grown out of the damaging misconception that the only alternative to a tightly controlled teacher led lesson involving reading, writing and answering questions is an 'all singing, all dancing' affair. Teachers who don't do what teachers have always done are 'progressive trendies' and the inevitable consequence is that children will run riot and standards will plummet. It is a myth generated and perpetuated by a lengthy debate about the way teachers should teach that is as polemic as it is misinformed.

The strategies that are outlined in this book, and they are by no means exhaustive, go some way to exploding this myth. Challenging and stretching children to enable them to learn effectively need not be achieved at the expense of control. There is no inevitability about it. Children can, if desired, be encouraged to think alone and in silence, as many of the techniques outlined in this book demonstrate. Nor do they necessarily take any longer than the activities they replace.

In many respects they appear to require only a slight variation in teaching style. Cosmetically, at least, this may be true but the shift in emphasis from receiving information to thinking about it and from answering questions to asking them is as fundamental as it is subtle.

Children deserve the best. Our job is not just to control them but to teach them. The National Curriculum is not for them to cover but to learn. We must strive to make our lessons extraordinary in every sense so that children leave them stimulated, enthused and eager to discover more. Above all, we must ensure that children leave our lessons knowing and understanding more than they did when they entered the room because quite simply that is what lessons are for - ah, but nothing!

Lessons are for Learning

THE SCHOOL EFFECTIVENESS SERIES

Lessons are for Learning is the fourth title in The School Effectiveness Series, which focuses on practical and useful ideas for schools and teachers. It addresses the issues of whole school improvement along with new knowledge about teaching and learning, while offering straightforward solutions which teachers can use to make life more rewarding for themselves and those they teach.

Book 1: *Accelerated Learning in the Classroom* by Alistair Smith
ISBN: 1855390345   £15.95

- The first book in the UK to apply new knowledge about the brain to classroom practice
- Contains practical methods so teachers can apply accelerated learning theories to their own classrooms
- Aims to increase the pace of learning and deepen understanding
- Includes advice on how to create the ideal environment for learning and how to help learners fulfil their potential
- Full of lively illustrations, diagrams and plans
- Offers practical solutions on improving performance, motivation and understanding
- Contains a checklist of action points for the classroom - 21 ways to improve learning

Book 2: *Effective Learning Activities* by Chris Dickinson
ISBN: 1855390353   £8.95

- An essential teaching guide which focuses on practical activities to improve learning
- Aims to improve results through effective learning, which will raise achievement, deepen understanding, promote self-esteem and improve motivation
- Includes activities which are designed to promote differentiation and understanding
- Offers advice on how to maximise the use of available - and limited - resources
- Includes activities suitable for GCSE, National Curriculum, Highers, GSVQ and GNVQ
- From the author of the highly acclaimed Differentiation: A Practical Handbook of Classroom Strategies

Book 3: *Effective Heads of Department* by Phil Jones & Nick Sparks
ISBN: 1855390361   £8.95

- An ideal support for Heads of Department looking to develop necessary management skills
- Contains a range of practical systems and approaches; each of the eight sections ends with a "checklist for action"
- Designed to develop practice in line with OFSTED expectations and DfEE thinking by monitoring and improving quality
- Addressees issues such as managing resources, leadership, learning, departmental planning and making assessment valuable
- Includes useful information for Senior Managers in schools who are looking to enhance the effectiveness of their Heads of Department

Book 5: *Effective Learning in Science* by Paul Denley and Keith Bishop
ISBN: 1855390395   £11.95

- A new book that looks at planning for effective learning within the context of science
- Encourages discussion about the aims and purposes in teaching science and the role of subject knowledge in effective teaching
- Tackles issues such as planning for effective learning, the use of resources and other relevant management issues
- Offers help in the development of a departmental plan to revise schemes of work, resources classroom strategies, in order to make learning and teaching more effective
- Ideal for any science department aiming to increase performance and improve results

Flexible Learning: Evidence Examined is a fascinating case study of flexible learning compared to a more formal teaching approach.

The book details a four-year pilot study in a comprehensive school in Cheltenham, where the author of the book - the Head of Geography - used flexible learning methods while colleagues taught the same curriculum more formally to pupils of similar ability.

They documented examination results, test scores, pupil behaviour and motivation, staying-on rates post-16 and allowed pupils and parents to offer their perceptions. The results are stunning.
The evidence is factual - and cannot be ignored.

An ideal starting point for discussion on teaching methods, *Flexible Learning: Evidence Examined* challenges the simplistic solutions to education issues from politicians and resists their suggestions for more testing and more whole-class teaching.

Mike Hughes focuses instead on the philosophy and practice of flexible learning, suggesting that the rationale of the teaching should be based on the small group tutorial and around individual
action plans.

> *"I hope that the book will stimulate interest in, and generate discussion about, effective classroom practice, so that ultimately, it may benefit those who matter the most - the pupils."*
>
> Mike Hughes, Acknowledgement to Flexible Learning: Evidence Examined, 1993

ISBN: 1855390132   £8.50   96pp

Flexible Learning: Evidence Examined is the fifth book in the Teaching and Learning Series.

Also available:

Flexible Learning: An Outline	by Philip Waterhouse	1855390035	£6.50
Classroom Management	by Philip Waterhouse	1855390043	£6.50
Resources for Flexible Learning	by Robert Powell	1855390051	£6.50
Tutoring	by Philip Waterhouse	185539006X	£6.50

For more details on these or any other publications from **Network Educational Press**, please contact us on 01785 225515 (Fax 01785 228566) or write to: PO Box 635, Stafford ST16 1BF.

* Please keep me informed of all future publications and special offers.